BASIC
Programming on the
BBC
Microcomputer

Contents

Preface

This book teaches the computer language BASIC, specially for the BBC Microcomputer. We have written it in non-technical language, assuming that you have no previous experience of computing and no special mathematical training. We start with a gently paced introduction and then go on to more sophisticated programming so that you can make the most of the various features of the computer and its BASIC. At every stage we actively involve you in your learning through frequent and clearly labelled activities on the computer.

Computing is fun! Whether you want to compute as a hobby, for business purposes or for teaching, we expect you to enjoy using this book. We certainly enjoyed writing it, not least because we were so impressed with the BBC Microcomputer! It was produced to link with the BBC television computer-literacy project, first broadcast early in 1982. It has a number of special features which are not available at the moment on other home-computers, and its BASIC includes advanced structures which are likely to have a wide and long-lasting impact. We explain how you can make the most of all these features and we try to instil good programming practice. We do this by example: we do not labour it, neither do we so condense our programs as to risk making their structure unclear.

The outstanding features of the BBC Microcomputer are the colour graphics, the animation and the sound.

In the colour graphics, eight flashing and eight non-flashing colours are available, and the resolution - i.e. the clarity of the picture - is second to that of no other home-computer on the market today. You can program the colour in a variety of ways, so that you can draw spectacular and colourful pictures and graphs. The animation facilities are fascinating and enable you to turn on and off and move parts of the picture. Hence you can program your own computer games. You can either control them using the keyboard or you can buy special levers to do it. These are known as 'paddles'.

The sound facility is something which you may like to use with games. You can program the notes yourself, controlling their pitch and how they build up and decay away. If you want, you can even program them to imitate particular musical instruments.

The computer offers other useful features. For example, when you make a mistake in programming, the computer writes the nature of your mistake on the screen as what is known as an 'error message'. Error messages are particularly clear on this computer because they are given as meaningful words, rather than as codes.

Also the editing is very good - particularly if you are a one-finger typist! Unlike with many home-computers, you don't have to retype the complete line every time you make a mistake. You need only retype the letters which are wrong.

BBC BASIC has a number of unique features which you will appreciate once you start programming: The AUTO line number and RENUMBER facilities are standard rather than extras. Also, in contrast with many home-computers, procedures are allowed as well as functions. Both can consist of more than one line and the variables can be declared as local to the particular procedure or function, which cuts down the likelihood of errors. The string search routine is also unusual and useful.

We owe a considerable debt of gratitude to many people without whose help the book could never have reached publication. To name just a few, our thanks are due to the Acorn staff for allowing one of us (Neil Cryer) to familiarize himself with a pre-production model of the microcomputer, especially to Roger Wilson who wrote the BASIC, to Peter Miller for help with the sound, and to Paul Bond. They patiently gave their time to discuss points and respond to queries. Our thanks are also due to the production team at the BBC who allowed one of us (Neil Cryer) to try out programs on its pre-production model. The self-study aspects of the book have benefited much from the association of one of us (Pat Cryer) with the education branch of a multi-national computing concern and with the Institute for Educational Technology at the University of Surrey. In particular we are grateful for help and advice from Professor Lewis Elton, head of the Institute. We are also grateful to Dr R. A. Brown and Nick Rose, both of Chelsea College, University of London, for helpful comments on early drafts. Andrew Cryer, our son, deserves special mention for his support and constructive criticism at all stages of the writing. We are also grateful to Wendy Cryer, our daughter, for drawing the cartoons. It is customary to conclude by thanking a typist for typing the manuscript - but we did our own typing. We are forever thankful for the existence of a word-processing package on our home personal computer!

Neil Cryer   Pat Cryer

London
February 1982

Cultivating an Acorn

0 Introduction

0.0 About this book

This book teaches the computer language BASIC with particular
reference to the BBC Microcomputer. Although you will still be able
to use it for an overview of BASIC if you do not have a
microcomputer, you will find it much easier if you have the BBC
machine. This is because we have written the book in such a way
that you will learn by doing, as well as by reading. We assume that
you are sitting at the computer as you read, and we break the text
up every few paragraphs with activities for you to try out.
      The book is divided into chapters. This one introduces you to
the machine and to our way of working. The second to the sixth

introduce some fundamentals of the BASIC language and are best read in order. Chapters 7, 8 and 9 introduce graphics and computer games, and Chapters 10, 11, 12, 13 and 14 deal with more sophisticated features of BASIC. Chapter 14 also gives an introduction to sound.

At the end of most chapters, to help you consolidate, we give some points for you to think about, and we follow with a discussion of how you might have set about them. In most chapters we also include a section of hints and discussion of the activities, particularly where they involve writing programs.

We now continue this chapter with a few short and simple sample sections to illustrate our mode of working. First are some sections in which we give information to you: about the advantages of programming in BASIC, about how to turn on the BBC Microcomputer and a few things which you can do to familiarize yourself with it. Next we give a short section of activities where it is your turn to do something yourself, and finally we give a very short section posing some simple points for you to think about, followed by an indication of how we see the answers.

0.1 Why program in BASIC?

You probably already realize what a huge impact computers are making on society. You may have seen them demonstrated on television or have played with them, perhaps in the form of space-invaders games. You probably feel that you would like to master them. This book is a step towards doing so.

Although a computer is a totally obedient servant, it has no intelligence of its own, and only does what it is told to do. In this book we shall be writing the instructions in the computing language BASIC, which has been created specifically for beginners. It is powerful enough for most purposes and yet is easy to pick up because it uses words which sound like everyday English.

In contrast with some computers, the BBC Microcomputer is ready to accept instructions in BASIC as soon as it is turned on.

0.2 Turning on the BBC Microcomputer

As we mentioned earlier, we are assuming that you have the BBC Microcomputer beside you and that you will try out most things as we introduce them - although we advise you to wait until the activities sections before doing so. If you have a different computer, there will inevitably be times when things do not happen exactly as we describe. All computers are slightly different, even to the extent of the type of BASIC they use and how they turn on.

Your first step will be to connect your computer to a television or a monitor as described in the User Guide - but please don't do this yet. When you have turned on and suitably tuned the television, the screen will display a prompt. It will be like one of the following, depending on your model of the BBC Microcomputer:

BBC Computer 16K

BASIC

or:
>_

BBC Computer 32K

BASIC
>_

The dash is called a 'cursor'; it flashes.

The prompt > shows that the computer is in the command mode and is ready for use. If at any stage some other message appears, showing that it is not in the command mode, perhaps because you have accidentally leant on the keyboard, you can get back into the command mode by pressing either the 'escape' key or the 'break' key. The escape key is on the left-hand side of the keyboard and the break key is on the top right-hand side of the keyboard.

Also when you turn on, a red light on the bottom left-hand side of the keyboard shows that 'caps lock' is active. This means that all typed letters come out as capitals, and that the keys displaying numbers and symbols give numbers. Capital (i.e. upper-case) letters are used more often in computing than non-capital (i.e. lower-case) letters.

0.3 Becoming familiar with the BBC Microcomputer

When you press a key to type, the character appears at the position of the cursor, and the cursor moves along as typing progresses.

The 'return' key, which is on the right of the keyboard, is important because the act of pressing it, which is called 'entering', signals your typed instruction to the computer. It indicates that you are satisfied that what you have typed is acceptable and that the computer should act on it. Right up until the time you press this key, you can alter the instruction as much as you like, so giving you the opportunity to change your mind and correct any typing mistakes. Corrections can be made using the 'delete' key, which is also on the right of the keyboard. It deletes one character at a time, to the left of the cursor, ready for retyping.

Now try the following activities.

0.4 Activities

---

i. Connect the BBC Microcomputer as described in the User Guide.

Turn it on and suitably tune the television. (A monitor will not require tuning.) Do you see one of the prompts mentioned in section 0.2? If not, reread the first few pages of the User Guide.

ii. Press any key or series of keys, including the space-bar at the front of the keyboard. Practise editing by using the delete key, and retyping. (Incidentally some of the keys with the more obscure symbols do not correspond with the display on the screen. This need not concern you at this stage.)

iii. Type in anything you like and enter it by pressing the return key. Do you get an error message? Press the escape key to get back into the command mode. Type and enter something again, but this time press the break key. What is the difference between the effects of these two keys? (See section 0.7 on page 5.)

iv. Disable caps lock by a single press of the 'caps lock' key, which is on the left of the keyboard. Does the red light go out? Now press some keys including a few with numbers on. What is the effect of typing with caps lock inactive? (We discuss this in section 0.7.) You can get caps lock operational once more by pressing the caps lock key again.

v. Press the 'shift lock' key which is on the left of the keyboard. What happens to the red light? Now press some keys, including a few with numbers on. What is the effect of typing with shift lock active? (We discuss this in section 0.7.) You can get out of shift lock by pressing the shift lock key again.

vi. With caps lock operational, press a 'shift' key. There are two: one at each side of the keyboard. While keeping it pressed, type something. Is the effect the same as with the shift lock? (See section 0.7.)

0.5 Some points to think about

a.   How do you prepare the BBC Microcomputer to accept comma in BASIC?

b.   What damage can be caused by pressing the wrong key?

0.6 Discussion on the points to think about

a.   In contrast with many other microcomputers, the BBC machine is ready to receive BASIC as soon as it is turned on. If it does not show the usual prompt at any stage, press the break key to return it to the command mode.

b. None. It is impossible to damage the machine by pressing the wrong key, although it can sometimes produce rather strange effects. When this happens you can normally recover by pressing the break key, although sometimes (when the computer is said to 'crash') it will not work properly until it is turned off and then turned on again.

0.7 Discussion of activities

0.4 iii. Both the escape key and the break key prepare the computer to receive new entries. With the break key, previous entries are lost, whereas with the escape key they are still displayed. You will probably prefer to use the escape key as it is helpful to be able to refer back to previous entries.

0.4 iv. With caps lock active, you get numbers and upper-case letters. This is the most useful combination for BASIC programming, so you will normally choose to have it on. Without caps lock, letters are in lower-case; numbers are unaffected.

0.4 v. With shift lock active, you get letters in upper-case and symbols instead of numbers. You will be using some of these symbols very frequently in BASIC programming. The red shift lock light indicates an active shift lock.

0.4 vi. You will certainly need symbols like #, $ and %. As you will normally have caps lock active, you will probably find it easier to get them using the shift key together with the appropriate key.

Entering programs

1   Starting programming

1.0 Immediate actions

There are some instructions which the computer responds to immediately you enter them. They are known as 'immediate actions'. The following is an example; it causes HELLO to appear on the screen:

    PRINT "HELLO"

HELLO may be described as a 'printout'. Alternatively it is said to be 'printed to the screen'.

The following immediate action causes the sum of 3 and 4 to be printed to the screen:

PRINT 3 + 4

Immediate actions can consist of more than one line. For example, if each of the following lines is typed and entered, in order, the sum of X and Y appears on the screen:

LET X=3
LET Y=4
PRINT X+Y

The following activities illustrate immediate actions.

1.1 Activities

---

i. Turn on the computer and type and enter the following. Remember to press the return key at the end of the line to signal that you are satisfied with it and that the computer should respond.

PRINT 458

Does 458 appear on the screen? If not, press the escape key and start again.

ii. Next you are going to ask the computer to do an addition. You will need to use the shift key to get the plus sign. Type and enter:

PRINT 5+9

Is 14 printed to the screen?

iii. Can you suggest whether or not you need the shift key to get a minus sign and an equals sign? Do a trial to see. Type and enter:

LET X=9
LET Y=45
PRINT Y-X

Is 36 printed to the screen?

1.2 What is a program?

A program is a set of instructions which the computer stores and

carries out as soon as you instruct it to by entering RUN. The
computer then 'executes' or 'runs' the program. Programs are not the
same as immediate actions which the computer responds to a line at
a time and, having done so, does not store.

Each line of a program begins with a line number which indicates
the sequence in which the computer should carry out the instruction.
The following is a simple BASIC program whose purpose is to take
two numbers and add them together.

```
1 LET X=45
2 LET Y=20
3 LET Z=X+Y
4 PRINT Z
5 END
```

When you feed this program into your computer, as you will be
invited to do shortly, the value of the sum of the two numbers will
appear on your screen.

The order in which the computer executes commands is dictated
by the line numbers which you supply. The computer always takes
them in line number sequence, irrespective of the order in which you
enter them. We will include an END statement with all complete
programs or sections of programs to distinguish them from example
lines. In practice the BBC Microcomputer does not give an error
message if an END statement is missed off; so you may treat it as
optional in your own programming.

In the following activities, you will be invited to enter our
simple program into your own computer, run it and to do what is
called 'listing' it. 'Listing' gets a copy of a program displayed on
the screen. To list, just type LIST and press the return key. The
program then appears on the screen.

For a long program, only a few lines can be displayed at a time;
so an extended form of the LIST command is required. For example,
to instruct the computer to display all the lines between line 6 and
line 12, type LIST 6,12. The first number is the line at which the
listing should start and the second is the last line to be listed. If
the line numbers do not exist, only the lines between appear on the
screen. You may interrupt a long listing and get back into the
command mode, by pressing the escape key.

Now a word of caution. In activities, we shall normally be
speaking about 'entering' commands or lines of program. As you
know, this means that you should type in the command or line and
then press the return key to enter it. From now on, though, we shall
not always be specifically reminding you to press this key; so make
a point of remembering. If you forget, your instruction will not be
received by the computer and nothing will happen.

1.3 Activities

---

i. With the computer in the command mode, enter each line of the program of section 1.2. Just type in the whole of each line, starting with the line number and finishing by pressing the return key. Each line of the program should then appear on a separate line on the screen, just as it is printed in this book.

ii. Enter LIST. Does a listing of the program appear on the screen? If not, was it because you forgot to press the return key to enter your typing? Check the program as listed on the screen. If any line is wrong, read the next section, which is on editing, and come back to this activity.

iii. Now run the program by typing and entering RUN. Does 65 appear on the screen? If not, there must be an error in your program. Read the next section and then try this activity again.

1.4 Some program editing commands

There are various ways you can alter or 'edit' a program.

You can remove a single line of program by merely typing and entering its line number. You can remove several lines at a time with the DELETE command, which needs to be typed in full - the delete key does not do the trick. The method is best explained by means of an example. Let us suppose that you wish to delete all the lines of a program between, say, line 5 and line 9. You can do this by typing and entering:

DELETE 5,9

If you should want to remove an entire program, you can do it by typing and entering the command NEW. A NEW command can be very annoying on some computers as it loses the program for ever. On the BBC Microcomputer, however, typing and entering OLD recovers the previous program, provided you have not meanwhile entered any new lines of program.

The BBC Microcomputer has a facility whereby it will automatically supply line numbers for you when you type and enter a program. It requires the command AUTO. Then every time you press the return key to enter a line, the next line number appears, ready for you. For example if you type and enter AUTO 1,3, the computer automatically numbers your program lines as you enter them, starting with line one and going up in increments of three. Thus the next line will be line 4 which will be followed by line 7 etc. To get out of this mode, once you have finished entering the program, press the escape key.

There will be many times when you will want to insert a new line of program between two existing ones. This is no problem if you get in the habit of numbering your lines in largish increments. Then there will always be spare numbers for new lines. We recommend starting at line 10 and going up in increments of ten. We can explain through the following example. Let us suppose that you have the following two lines of program:

```
10 LET X=2.5
20 PRINT Z
```

Let us also suppose that you wish to insert two lines to make the program similar to that of section 1.2. You can enter the following two lines:

```
14 LET Y=55
16 LET Z=X+Y
```

You do not have to insert them in order because, as you will remember, BASIC always sorts lines into order of ascending line number. In the following activities, you will be invited to check this by listing.

This method of adding extra lines can still run into trouble if very many are to be added to the middle of an existing program. Then the program needs a new set of line numbers. The BBC Microcomputer has a command for this, called RENUMBER. Entering, for example, RENUMBER 10,20 causes the program lines to be renumbered starting at line number 10 with an increment of twenty from one line number to the next.

1.5 Activities

---

i. With the machine in the command mode, enter the program in section 1.2. Type and enter LIST to list the program to check that it is there.

ii. Try entering 1. Then list the program again and see what is missing. Do you find that line 1 is missing?

iii. Use this technique to remove the entire program and then enter the same program again, this time entering line 5 first followed by lines 4,3,2 and 1. List your program. Have the lines been put back into order?

iv. Enter NEW. Then enter LIST. Does this remove your program?

v. Enter OLD. Then enter LIST. Does your old program reappear?

vi. Press the break key. Then enter LIST. Does the program
disappear? Does OLD bring it back again? Now press the escape
key. How is its effect different from that of the break key? (See
section 1.8.)

vii. Use the AUTO command to enter the program in section 1.2
with the same set of line numbers. List the program to be sure that
they are correct. Then use the RENUMBER command to give line
numbers starting at 10 with increments of 10. List your program
again. Have the lines been renumbered?

viii. Use the DELETE command to remove the lines which were 2
and 3 but are now 20 and 30. Then try to run your program. Why is
there an error message? (See section 1.8.)

1.6 Some points to think about

a. What is a computer program?
b. What happens if you enter a program line with a previously
   used line number?
c. What happens if you enter program lines in the reverse order to
   their line numbers?
d. What happens if you type NEW followed by a new program
   line?

1.7 Discussion on the points to think about

a. A computer program is a sequence of instructions written
   in a language that the computer can recognize and obey.
   There are of course other ways of saying this.
b. The second line replaces the first.
c. The computer stores the lines, then lists and executes them in
   the order of the line numbers. The order of entry is
   immaterial.
d. The old program is lost and the new line is accepted as the
   first for the new program.

1.8 Discussion of activities

1.5 vi. Both the escape and the break keys stop the execution of any
program, but whereas the break key clears the screen, the escape key
merely prepares the computer for new instructions while still
displaying the current program. Having pressed the break key, you
can still get your old program back by typing OLD, provided that you

have not entered any new program.

1.5 viii. The error message arises because the program tries to print a value for Z before any value has been given to it. Error messages are useful because they indicate the nature of programming errors, which is the first step to putting them right.

Executing programs

2 More simple programming

2.0 The PRINT statement

The PRINT statement is so common in programming that it is very important to become thoroughly familiar with what it does, and fully

13

confident in using it yourself. As you have seen already, a line such as 40 PRINT X causes the computer to print whatever value it holds for X. With several PRINT statements, the result of each is normally given on a new line. This is true even if the PRINT statement appears with no instruction as to what to print. So a blank PRINT statement causes a move to the next line. Let us look at the following program as an example:

```
10 LET A=4
20 PRINT A
30 PRINT
40 PRINT
50 PRINT
60 PRINT A
70 END
```

This causes the screen to display the value of A twice with three blank lines between them. So a program with a sufficient number of empty PRINT statements would clear the screen - although, as you will see, this is not the simplest way to do it.

If you want to print two values on the same line, with no spaces between them, you can indicate this in the PRINT statement by inserting a semicolon between the two numbers. For example the following line causes the two values, 12 and 35, to appear together as 1235 with no intervening spaces:

```
20 PRINT 12;35
```

Regarding spaces, the BBC Microcomputer prints the minus sign for negative numbers but otherwise puts the numbers as close together as possible.

2.1 Activities

_____

Examine the following short program and decide what you think it will print on the screen when it is run:

```
10 LET P = 44
20 LET Q = 2
30 PRINT P;Q-P;Q
40 END
```

Enter the program, run it and see if you were right.

_____

2.2 Tabulation: TAB and the comma

If you want to control whereabouts the numbers appear in a line of printing, you can do it by means of a TAB instruction. The following is an example:

    30 PRINT TAB(20);A

This prints out spaces ending at the 20th character position, and then prints the value of A. The number in brackets after the word TAB gives the character position to be moved to, numbering from the left, and you can of course vary it. For example, the following lines produce three columns with two numbers in each:

    20 PRINT A;TAB(15);B;TAB(30);C
    30 PRINT X;TAB(15);Y;TAB(30);Z

If the printing has already proceeded beyond the character position requested by the TAB statement, printing moves onto the beginning of the next line before writing in the required spaces.

    The use of TAB followed by a semicolon allows you to fix where numbers start in a line of printing. For example, the two lines

    10 PRINT 32;TAB(14);45;TAB(20);6
    20 PRINT 6;TAB(14);3;TAB(20);67

produce the following alignment in which units are in the same columns as tens:

    32   45   6
    6   3   67

    It is more usual to want numbers aligned like this with all the tens in one column and the units in another column:

    32   45   6
    6   3   67

BBC BASIC provides for such a printout by means of a comma in the PRINT statement:

    10 PRINT 32,45,6
    20 PRINT 6,3,67

    It is useful to think of the screen as divided into zones which are ten characters wide. A comma in the PRINT statement causes the number after it to be printed as far to the right as possible in the next available zone. So the first number printed on a line is automatically placed to the right of the first zone. To get it at the start of a line requires a semicolon before the number. For example:

```
10 PRINT ;245
```

will produce:

245

2.3 Activities

---

i. To illustrate the use of the TAB statement, enter the following program:

```
10 LET A=120
20 LET B=435
30 LET C=B/A
40 PRINT A;TAB(15);B;TAB(25);C
50 PRINT A;TAB(15);B;TAB(25);C
60 END
```

Run the program by typing and entering RUN. Does it produce three columns of numbers across the screen?

ii. Try changing TAB(25) to TAB(10) and run the program. Why is the value of C printed on the next line? (See the previous section.)

iii. To illustrate the effect of commas in a PRINT statement, enter and run the following program:

```
10 LET A=651372
20 LET B=23
30 LET C=4
40 PRINT A,A,A
50 PRINT B,B,B
60 PRINT C,C,C
70 END
```

In the printout, are the right-hand sides of all the digits aligned?

iv. Next add the following lines to the program:

```
70 PRINT ;A;A,A
80 PRINT ;B;A,A
90 PRINT ;C;A,A
100 END
```

Run this program. Do you see the compression caused by the semicolons? Do you see the first number printed at the start of the line? Do you also see that the comma causes the number after it to be printed in the next available zone, provided this has sufficient space left?

2.4 More about the PRINT statement

Normally each PRINT statement causes printing on a new line. However, values contained in several PRINT statements can be printed on the same line if all but the final one ends with a semicolon or comma. Such PRINT statements may be separated by many program lines. For example, the following program would produce only one line of printout:

```
10 LET A=2
20 PRINT A;
30 LET B=1234
40 PRINT B
50 END
```

The program would print 2 on the right of the first ten-character zone and then, because of the semicolon, would not move on to a new line. Line 40 would then cause 1234 to be printed as far to the right as possible in the second zone. As no semicolon or comma appears at the end of line 40, any further print statements would produce printing on a new line.

You can force the printout to a new line within a single PRINT statement by using an apostrophe. For example the following program:

```
10 LET A = 2
20 LET B = 123
30 PRINT A,B'A,B
40 END
```

gives the printout:

```
2       123
2       123
```

2.5 Strings

We shall now introduce one of the simplest methods of printing messages. The message merely needs to be enclosed in double quotation marks in a PRINT statement, like this:

```
10 PRINT "THE SUM OF 2 AND 3 IS"
```

Then, when the program is run, the message between the quotes is printed on the screen.

Sometimes you may want the message to be in lower-case, like this:

    10 PRINT "The sum of 2 and 3 is"

You will remember that you can get lower-case by pressing the caps lock key once before typing.

Clearly, this use of the PRINT statement makes it much easier to present the results of calculations in an understandable way. The set of characters between the quotes is called a 'string'. The BBC Microcomputer always prints a string without any spaces before or after it. Hence a semicolon between strings causes them to be joined up when they are printed, as you can see in the next activities.

A PRINT statement like that in line 10 makes the printout start at the beginning of a line. There is no automatic insetting for a string as there is for a number.

2.6 Activities

----

i. Try entering and running the following program:

    10 LET A=23
    20 LET B=11
    30 LET S=A+B
    40 PRINT "The sum is ";S
    50 END

Do you see how you can use strings to present the results of programs in such a way that other people can know what the program has done or what the result means?

ii. Try replacing line 40 with:

    40 PRINT "The sum ";"is ";S

Run the program. Is an identical result produced? Does the semicolon cause the two strings to be printed out with no extra spaces between them?

iii. By using a long string made up of numbers, you can produce a program which more clearly demonstrates the effect of commas. Enter and run the following program:

    10 PRINT"123456789012345678901234567890012"
    20 PRINT 12,345,45
    30 PRINT 1,23,345

        40 END

Do you see that the first line prints out a whole string of numbers across the screen which can be used to count the column position of the numbers printed by lines 20 and 30? Are the numbers written by lines 20 and 30 aligned at columns 10, 20 and 30?

iv. Try entering the following program:

        10 PRINT "12345678901234567890"
        20 PRINT "cheers","cheers"
        30 END

Do you see that strings are printed on the left of a print zone?

———

2.7 The LET statement

You have seen that the LET statement gives a numerical value to a variable, as for example in LET X=2 or in LET S=X+Y. It is, however, not quite as obvious as it seems at first sight, because of the confusion of the statement looking like an equation. It is not an equation. In fact it is best to think of a LET statement as instructing, 'work out a numerical value for what is on the right and give it to the variable on the left'. We can explain by considering a LET statement that is perfectly valid, even though it may strike you as strange if you are used to dealing with equations:

        10 LET C=C+1

This merely commands the computer to take whatever value it holds for C, add 1 to it, and give it to the variable on the left. So, every time the statement is executed, the previous value of C is increased by 1. In practice this type of program line is useful for counting the number of times a statement is executed.
        The BBC BASIC allows you to leave out the word LET from the LET statement to save time in typing. So far, we have always inserted it, but only so as not to confuse you. From now on, though, we shall normally be leaving it out. So make sure that you are ready for statements that look like equations but are really LET statements. Here are some examples to get you used to the idea:

        10 X=45
    and
        12 S=X+Y
    and
        200 A=A+10

2.8 Variable names

We have been using symbols like A,B,C and X,Y,Z to represent
numerical values in the computer. As these symbols represent values
which can vary, they are known as 'variable names'. The BBC
Microcomputer is very unusual in that it accepts variable names of
any length. They may consist of upper-case letters, lower-case
letters, numbers and the underline character, but BASIC requires
them to start with a letter. Characters such as & or # are not
permitted. Every character in the variable name is significant. For
example, Average2 is perceived as different from Average3. Other
computers more usually distinguish only the first two letters in a
variable name.

We recommend that you use lower-case for all variable names
because otherwise the computer tends to get confused with BASIC
terms, e.g. it does not accept PRINTER because of its confusion
with PRINT.

It is very useful indeed to be able to represent variables with
names rather than as, say, X or Y. It makes the program easier to
read and therefore easier to check. To illustrate this, consider the
following program which has been written in two ways, the second
with meaningful words as variable names, and the first with letters.
As a variable name cannot contain a space, the words have to be
joined in some way. We have used the underline character to
represent a space. Apart from in variable names and strings, BASIC
ignores extra spaces. So we shall often be putting them in to make
programs look more attractive and readable. We do this here in the
right-hand version:

```
10 A = 5.56          10 oil_filter    = 5.56
20 B =12.30          20 oil           =12.30
30 C =18.64          30 labour        =18.64
40 D = 5.00          40 deposit       = 5.00
50 E = A+B+C-D       50 bill = oil_filter+oil+labour
60 PRINT E              -deposit
70 END               60 PRINT bill
                     70 END
```

Anyone can see immediately that the second program is to
calculate the cost of three items, an oil filter, oil and labour, and
that due allowance is to be made for the deposit paid. The first
program is nowhere near as clear. If it contained any errors, they
would be much more difficult to spot.

2.9 Activities
----

i. Enter and run the program on the right in the previous section.

ii. Now try putting more spaces into the program, and see just where they can go without causing error messages when the program is run.

iii. Will the following program run?

```
10 oil_filter = 5.56
20           oil =12.30
30         labour =18.64
40         deposit = 5.00
50 bill = oil_filter + oil + labour - deposit
60 PRINT "Nett garage bill =£";bill
70 END
```

iv. Suppose you replace line 10 by:

```
10 oil filter = 5.56
```

Will it be accepted? (This is dealt with in section 2.14 d.)

v. Try running the following program:

```
10 DELETER=45
20 PRINTER=3
30 PRINT DELETER+PRINTER
40 END
```

Why is there an error message? (See section 2.15.)

2.10 Integer variables

The variables that we have used so far can take any value, positive or negative - as long as it is between zero and ten raised to the thirty eighth power, i.e. 1 followed by 38 zeroes! BBC BASIC has another type of variable, which can take only integers, i.e. whole numbers. It is called an integer variable and is written as a normal variable name followed by a percentage sign, e.g. People%, CARS%, NUM%, G% etc. As an illustration of its use, consider the following program:

```
10 X = 4.99
20 Y% = X
30 PRINT Y%
40 END
```

The printout is 4 because the computer leaves off any fractional part of an integer variable. This means that 4.9 is not rounded to the nearest integer, but loses its fractional part. The value for Y% could be made equal to the rounded value of X by the following replacement line 20:

        20 Y% = X + 0.5

The use of integer variables can make programs faster and use less memory space, but you will probably find this negligible in most of your programs. They are also used when it is important not to have any small fractional parts, or to control the number of decimal places to be printed out.

2.11 String variables

BASIC not only allows variables to represent numbers, it also allows them to represent strings. When a variable is used in this way, it is known as a 'string variable'. It can be represented by any letter or name, but BASIC requires that it be immediately followed by a dollar sign, as for example in the following, where the word LET is of course optional and would normally be omitted:

        200 LET X$ = "John"

Line 60 of the program in section 2.9 caused a message to be printed on the screen by the use of a string in the PRINT statement. Alternatively, a string variable could have been used. Then the following two lines of program could have replaced line 60:

        60 message$="Nett garage bill =£"
        70 PRINT message$;bill

Then everything between the quotes would have been printed exactly word for word and, because of the semicolon, the value of bill would have been printed immediately after the string. So the printout would have read:

        Nett garage bill =£31.50

It is sometimes useful to be able to join strings together. A plus sign is all that is required. This may be thought of as adding two string variables - but they cannot of course be subtracted. Examples of suitable program lines could be:

        80 LET A$=B$+C$+D$
and
        85 LET PHRASE$="JACK"+" AND "+"JILL"
and
        82 LET EX$="HELLO "+B$+"."

You can practise this type of manipulation in the following activities.

2.12 Activities

----

i. Try entering and running the following program:

```
10 STR1$ = "NASA"
20 STR2$ = " space "
30 STR3$ = "shuttle"
40 PHRASE$ = STR1$ + STR2$ + STR3$
50 PRINT STR1$
60 PRINT STR2$
70 PRINT STR3$
80 PRINT PHRASE$
90 END
```

ii. What happens when you run the program with the following new line 20?

```
20 STR2$ = "space"
```

iii. Try running the program with line 80 changed to:

```
80 PRINT STR1$;STR2$;STR3$
```

Is there any change in the printout?

2.13 Some points to think about

a. Consider the following short program:

```
10 A = 352
20 B = 2
30 PRINT"123456789012345678901234567890 12"
40 PRINT B,A,"cheers";A
50 PRINT A,B,"cheers";B
60 END
```

Without running the program, can you work out the appearance of the printout?

b. Consider the following two short programs:

```
10 A = 32145        and        10 A$ = "32145"
20 PRINT A,A                   20 PRINT A$,A$
```

30 END   30 END

Would there be any difference in their displays?
c. How would the printout from the two programs differ if a
    semicolon replaced the comma in the PRINT statements?
d. Where is it not permissible to include spaces in a program?
e. Which of the following variable names are invalid in BASIC?

                    WOOD_price
                    3D
                    Y1
                    sex?
                    cost£
                    TAX$
                    TAX$CODE
                    LISTER

2.14 Discussion on the points to think about

a. The appearance of the printout would be as follows:

123456789012345678901234567890012
        2   352cheers352
        352   2cheers2

The first number to be printed in each PRINT statement is
automatically printed aligned on the right of the first print
zone. The second column is aligned because of the comma. The
fourth column is joined onto the third because of the
semicolon.
b. Yes. The first string is printed starting at the beginning of
    the line whereas the first number is printed aligned at the
    right of the first print zone. The second string and the
    second number is printed according to the comma, i.e.
    aligned to the left of the next available print zone for
    the string and to the right for the number.
c. The inclusion of the semicolon in the modified program causes
    the printout of the strings to be joined together starting at
    the beginning of the line like this:

3214532145

The numbers are also printed joined together but with the first
one printed to the right of the first print zone as follows:

32145

The second number is printed immediately afterwards to give:

32145 32145

d. Spaces can be put anywhere except that:

- Extra spaces in a string are part of it and thus alter how the string reads.
- Spaces are not permissible in variable names.
- Spaces are not permissible within a BASIC statement, for example as in PR INT for PRINT or LE T for LET.

e. The underline character is permissible. So WOOD_price is permissible. 3D starts with a number and is invalid. Y1 is valid. sex? contains a query which is invalid. The £ symbol is accepted if it is at the end of a variable name. Therefore cost£ is valid. TAX$ is valid for a string variable. TAX$CODE is invalid because of the imbedded $. LISTER starts with the BASIC term LIST and is therefore invalid.

2.15 Discussion of activities

2.9 v. The computer does not accept DELETER or PRINTER because they start with DELETE and PRINT respectively. It would not matter if the variable names contained these words, e.g. ZDELETE and JPRINTER would be accepted.

The escape key

3 Input statements and mathematics in programs

3.0 Introduction

You have now reached the stage where you need some elementary mathematics to develop your programming skills. We thought you would find this easier and more fun if you learnt it at the same time as practising it in programs. Consequently this chapter deals with how to input data into programs as well as how to cope with mathematics.

3.1 Simple arithmetic operations

Many programs involve calculations. There are five fundamental arithmetic operations. As you can see from Table 3.1, their symbols are very similar to those of ordinary arithmetic. The exceptions are for multiplication and raising to a power. The first modification prevents confusion with the letter x and the second arises because there is no way of writing a number above a line.

OPERATION	SYMBOL	EXAMPLE		
Addition	+	a+b	eg 3+2	(=5)
Subtraction	-	a-b	eg 3-2	(=1)
Multiplication	*	a*b	eg 3*2	(=6)
Division	/	a/b	eg 3/2	(=1.5)
Raising to a power	^	a^b	eg 3^2	(=9)

Table 3.1

It is important that the * symbol for multiplication is inserted between all symbols or numbers that are multiplied together. For example, 3 multiplied by b, which you are probably used to writing as 3b, has to be written as 3*b.

b^2 must be written as b^2.

3.2 Priorities of order in arithmetic

Sometimes, working out the value of an expression involves several separate, smaller calculations. You will recall from mathematics, that such expressions have to be treated in a certain order, e.g. brackets must be worked out first. If you get the order wrong, then the final answer is also wrong. The same is true in computing. To avoid any ambiguities, BASIC has rules of priority for dealing with calculations. It always performs operations in the following order:

FIRST   Evaluating a bracket or brackets (innermost first)

SECOND   Raising to a power

THIRD   Multiplication and division

FOURTH   Addition and subtraction

If operations of the same priority appear more than once on the same line, BASIC deals with them from left to right.

We shall illustrate by means of an example. First, one without brackets. Consider the expression:

$$3*Y\wedge2 + 5 \qquad \text{where Y has the value 4.}$$

As there are no brackets, there is no first priority operation. The next priority operation concerns the power; so the expression reduces to:

$$3*16 + 5$$

Since the next priority operation concerns multiplication and division, the expression next reduces to:

$$48 + 5$$

Since the last priority operation concerns addition and subtraction, the final answer is:

$$53$$

Now consider another expression which, incidentally, has the same numbers. The only difference is that there are brackets:

$$3*Y\wedge(2 + 5)$$

Since the first priority operation concerns brackets, and 3+5=7, the expression reduces to:

$$3*Y\wedge7$$

As Y has the value of 4, the next stage gives:

$$3*16384$$

The final answer is: 49152

The different answers to these two examples are entirely due to the order of performing the operations.

We now give some example expressions in ordinary mathematics and show their BASIC equivalents:

IN MATHEMATICS	IN BASIC		
$a(b+c)$	$a*(b+c)$	eg $2*(3+1)$	$(=8)$
$ab^2 + 45$	$a*b\wedge2 + 45$	eg $2*3\wedge2+45$	$(=63)$
$(x+y)^2$	$(x+y)\wedge2$	eg $(2+3)\wedge2$	$(=25)$

You may have noticed that when you carry on typing, the display spills over to make another line when it reaches the right-hand edge of the screen. Irrespective of how many screen lines are occupied, BASIC still regards the typing as a single program line until the return key is pressed. Each mathematical expression has to be written on a single program line, which can be up to 240 characters and is much longer than a screen line. With lengthy expressions this can make for difficult reading.

3.3 Activities

----

i. Enter and run the following program:

```
10 X=2
20 Y=3
30 PRINT X*Y+4
40 END
```

Note the answer that is displayed.

ii. Change line 30 to:

```
30 PRINT X*(Y+4)
```

Now run the program again. What is the answer now? Why are these answers different? (See section 3.10.)

iii. Change line 30 to:

```
30 PRINT (X*Y)+4
```

Run the program. What is the new answer? (Reasons for these variations are discussed in section 3.10.)

3.4 The INPUT statement

You are now familiar with the use of LET statements to give values to variables at the stage of typing in the program, before running it. We now deal with a method of giving values to variables while the program is running. The method uses what is called an INPUT statement. The INPUT statement causes the computer to stop execution of the program and display '?' followed by the cursor. Anything typed and entered at this stage is given to the variable in the INPUT statement. This is best illustrated by an example:

```
10 INPUT A$
20 PRINT A$
30 END
```

When the program runs, line 10 causes the screen to display ? and the cursor. Suppose you type in:

HELLO THERE

Once this is entered, the program continues - in this case, with HELLO THERE being printed to the screen.

Whenever you write a program which requires you or someone else to type and enter information while the program is running, it is a good idea to make the request appear on the screen in the form of a message. One way is to use a PRINT statement just before the INPUT statement. Another way is by means of a small extension to the INPUT statement. The message to be displayed is put within quotes like this:

```
10 INPUT"What is your name",name$
```

This line would display the prompt 'What is your name?'. The ? is supplied by the computer which then waits for a keyboard entry for the string variable name$.

There are times when it would be better not to have the question mark. This can be arranged by not putting a comma between the message in quotes and the variable name. For example:

```
10 INPUT "Type a message "A$
```

The following activities familiarize you with the message facility in the INPUT statement and the control of the question mark.

3.5 Activities

Enter and run the following program, and put in appropriate responses:

```
10 INPUT "Who am I talking to",name$
20 PRINT "Thank you ";name$
30 INPUT "How are you feeling today",answer$
40 PRINT name$;" I note you are feeling ";answer$
50 INPUT "Please type in anything "M$
60 PRINT M$
70 END
```

3.6 More about the INPUT statement

The INPUT statement can be used to give values to more than one variable. For example the following single line requires values for three string variables:

        10 INPUT A$,B$,C$

(The resulting ? and cursor do not indicate how many responses the computer expects. So it is important that there be a prompt.)

All three responses may be typed on the same line, separated from each other by commas. A comma, used in this way, is called a 'delimiter'. The computer uses it to identify where one string ends and the next starts. By way of illustration, imagine the following INPUT statement:

        10 INPUT"Type your name and sex"name$,sex$

If, in response to the prompt, "Type your name and sex", you type and enter:

        JILL,FEMALE

then the strings available in the program would be identical to those from the following LET statements:

        20 LET name$ = "JILL"
        30 LET sex$ = "FEMALE"

If you type and enter more strings than the computer expects in response to a particular INPUT statement, the extra values are ignored. If you type and enter too few items, the computer responds with a question mark on the next line. You then merely have to type and enter the extra; the computer has already accepted the earlier ones.

The same form of the INPUT statement may be used for a numerical input, with numerical variables. For example, the following program would ask for two numbers to be typed in, and would then cause their sum to be printed:

        10 INPUT"Type in two numbers"N1,N2
        20 sum=N1+N2
        30 PRINT "THE SUM IS ";sum
        40 END

Once again the numbers should be typed with commas between them, and if too few are entered, the computer prints another question mark. If too many are entered, the extra are ignored.

Although there is no problem with using the INPUT statement with a mixture of numerical and string variables, you must ensure that each variable receives the value expected by the program. If you enter a number for a string, there is no problem except that you must only handle it as a string. You could not do any arithmetic with it. If, however, you enter a string for a numerical variable, although there will be no error message, there is clearly an error. We can illustrate by considering the following INPUT statement:

```
10 INPUT"Type your name and age separated by a
   comma "name$,age
```

The required responses would of course be something like:

```
PETER,15
```

Suppose, however, that these were typed in the wrong order by mistake:

```
15,PETER
```

The 15 would be perfectly acceptable as a value for the string variable name$, but PETER would give a value of 0 for age.

3.7 Activities

----

i. To practise the use of messages in the INPUT statement, enter and run the following simple maths program, and put in appropriate responses:

```
10 INPUT "Type two numbers separated by a comma "N1,N2
20 sum     = N1 + N2
30 product = N1 * N2
40 PRINT "THE SUM =";sum
50 PRINT "THE PRODUCT =";product
60 END
```

ii. What response do you get if you enter 15,TEN in answer to the request for two numbers in the program above? (We discuss this in section 3.10.)

iii. To illustrate the use of strings in an INPUT statement, enter the following program:

```
10 INPUT"Type three strings separated by commas "A$,B$,C$
20 PRINT A$
30 END
```

Run the program several times, each time typing and entering various combinations for the response. Try whatever you think will enable you to answer the following questions:

1. Is only the first string printed each time?

2. Can you get the final printed message without entering three strings either on one line separated by commas or on three separate lines?

3. If too many strings are typed in, is an error message displayed?

4. Are numbers an acceptable response for this particular program? (See section 3.10.)

iv. The following program illustrates the use of mixed string and numerical variables in an INPUT statement. Enter and run it.

```
10 INPUT"TYPE NAME, AGE, AND TWO NUMBERS"
   name$,age,num1,num2
20 sum=num1+num2
30 PRINT"HELLO ";name$;" THE SUM OF YOUR
   NUMBERS IS ";sum
40 END
```

What variations of response can you type without getting an error message?

v. Try typing and entering a single response. Note the display and then type and enter the next response.

vi. What is the result of entering something like:

STUPID COMPUTER,GO AWAY,2,2

(See section 3.10.)

vii. Try writing a program to calculate the number of rolls of wallpaper to cover a room with one door and one window. Get the program to ask for the size of the room, and the size of the door and the window - which will of course not need to be covered. Calculate the number of rolls on the basis of their being equal to the number of times the area to be covered is greater than the area of a single roll. (We give a simple program in section 3.10.) Our program does not allow for wastage due to pattern matching and unusable short pieces of wallpaper. How could such factors be allowed for?

3.8 Some points to think about

a. How would the following expressions have to be written for a
    BASIC program?

    (a) $3C(A+B)^2$ (b) AX^2+BX+C (c) $(X+Y)AB^2$

b. The following INPUT statement is part of a program:

    300 INPUT "Type Name and Number",name$,num

    For each of the responses given below, will the program

    -   run correctly
    -   run incorrectly
    -   give an error message but continue and run correctly
    -   give an error message and require a completely new
        response
    -   give an error message and require extra information?

            BRICKS 52,000
            HAY,284,BALES
            PETER,24
            CUPS,284 BROKEN
            JOHN

c. Write a program that will ask for a number, and then print that
    number followed by an appropriate message and the number
    squared.
d. Write a program to print out the value of the square of $(B+1)$
    for a value of B obtained as the result of an INPUT
    statement.

3.9 Discussion on the points to think about

a. The multiplication signs and the raise to power signs must be
    inserted, giving:

    (a) $3*C*(A+B)\wedge2$ (b) $A*X\wedge2+B*X+C$ (c) $(X+Y)*A*B\wedge2$

b. BRICKS 52,000 runs incorrectly if the required number was
    52000 and BRICKS was the name.
    HAY,284,BALES runs correctly. The extra is ignored.
    PETER,24 runs correctly.
    CUPS,284 BROKEN runs correctly as the space after 284
    is taken as the end of the number. BROKEN is ignored.
    JOHN just causes a question mark to be printed showing
    that more information is to be entered.
c. Programs can be written many different ways. We give two

possible versions, but yours may differ from either and still be right.

```
10 INPUT "Give me a number",number
20 PRINT number;
30 square=number*number
40 PRINT "squared =";square
50 END
```

or

```
10 INPUT "Give me a number",N
20 PRINT N;" squared =";N*N
30 END
```

d. Again, we give two alternatives, but there are many more:

```
10 INPUT "Enter B ",B
20 X = (B + 1)∧2
30 PRINT "The answer is "; X
40 END
```

or

```
10 INPUT "Type B"B
20 result = (B+1)∧2
30 PRINT "Value of (B+1)∧2 is ";result
40 END
```

3.10 Discussion of activities

3.3 i, ii and iii. The second answer is different from the first because the brackets change the priority of working. The last answer should be the same as the first because, although the bracket caused X*Y to be evaluated first, this was the order of priority anyway. So the brackets had no effect.

3.7 ii. The string TEN entered in response to a request for a number results in the numerical variable being given the value 0. The sum then becomes 15 and the product 0.

3.7 iii. 1. Yes.

2. No. You will find that you have to provide values for all the variables in the INPUT statement before the computer will proceed to the next line of program.

3. The BBC Microcomputer gives no error message if too many items are entered in response to an INPUT statement.

4. Numbers are perfectly acceptable values to be entered for a string variable in an INPUT statement.

3.7 vi. If strings are found when numerical values are expected, no error message is issued. So be careful how you write your program. Always make sure that anyone who runs it can know exactly what he or she should enter.

3.7 vii. One version of the program to calculate the number of rolls of wallpaper is as follows:

```
 10 PRINT"Enter length, breadth and height of"
 20 PRINT"room separated by commas. NOTE"
 30 PRINT"you MUST use either metres OR feet"
 40 PRINT"and only decimal fractions of these."
 50 INPUT"e.g. 8.2,10.5,11"length,breadth,height
 60 area = 2*(length+breadth)*height
 70 PRINT"Enter the width, height of door."
 80 INPUT width,height
 90 area=area - width*height
100 PRINT "Enter the width, height of window."
110 INPUT width,height
120 area=area-width*height
130 PRINT"Enter the length and breadth of the"
140 INPUT"wallpaper roll in same units "length,breadth
150 roll_area = length*breadth
160 PRINT
170 PRINT"The number of rolls required is ";
    area/roll_area
180 END
```

Saving programs

4 Branching

4.0 Introduction

Computers execute a program a line at a time, in line number
sequence. So the lines have to be numbered in the order that you
want them executed. Sometimes, however, it is useful for the order
of execution to depend on the values being processed by the program.
Such changing of the order of execution is called 'branching'.

4.1 The GOTO statement

The GOTO statement is the simplest way of forcing the computer to
execute a program in an order other than the line numbers dictate.
It is an instruction to jump or branch to a new line somewhere else.
For example the following line causes the computer to continue
execution at line 200:

        100 GOTO 200

The BBC BASIC allows jumping to, say, line X, where X is
calculated by the computer from the information that you feed into
it. The following would be an appropriate instruction, provided that
the previous part of the program calculates X:

        110 GOTO X

Although the RENUMBER command renumbers the 200 in line
100 above, it cannot renumber the X in line 110. You should
therefore restrict such use of GOTO.
    You will frequently want the computer to perform the same task
repetitively. This requires a backwards jump as instructed by the
following line of program:

        130 GOTO 10

You should be careful in using such statements. Unless you
include appropriate limiting instructions somewhere else in the
program, you may find the computer executing an endless loop which
will go on forever unless you press the escape key.
    If you prematurely stop a program by pressing the escape key,
you can restart it by typing and entering either RUN or GOTO.
    RUN causes execution from the first line of the program, i.e.
the program executes as if it had never been run before.
    GOTO 10 causes the program to begin execution at the given
line number (in this case 10). This allows the program to carry on
executing with all variables still holding their current values.

4.2 Activities

---

i. Enter the following program:

```
10 num = num + 1
20 PRINT num,"Hello I am a computer"
30 GOTO 10
```

(Incidentally we have not bothered to put in a final line saying END because the computer can never reach it.)

Run this program. Is the computer in a never-ending loop?

ii. Press the escape key and note that the program stops running.

iii. Enter either RUN or GOTO 10, and then stop the program again by pressing the escape key. Repeat this as often as you need in order to see the differences between these two methods of starting a program. (See section 4.17 for a comment.)

4.3 Conditional branching and comparisons

The computer is well suited for making arithmetic decisions, and indeed without this facility it would be of little use. At various stages in a program you may want the processing to depend on the result of a decision - for instance you may want the computer to take in data until no more is available, and then do some calculation. In such a case the computer has to decide when all the data is in. So the program must test this and branch accordingly. This sort of branching is called 'conditional branching' in contrast with our previous branching which has been 'unconditional'.

Conditional branching involves comparisons, of which there are several types. BASIC requires each to be represented by its own sign as listed below.

COMPARISON	SIGN
equals	=
not equal to	<>
less than	<
greater than	>
less than or equal to	<=
greater than or equal to	>=

4.4 The IF . . THEN statement

The IF . . THEN construction allows the computer to make a
decision or come to a conclusion. If the condition given by the IF is
satisfied, the computer executes according to what follows the
THEN. If the condition is not satisfied, the rest of the line is
ignored and the computer moves onto the next line. As an
illustration, consider the following program which keeps asking for a
number:

```
10 INPUT"Type in a number "N
20 IF N=2 THEN PRINT"That was two"
30 GOTO 10
```

If 2 is entered, the computer will reply: 'That was two' and then
carry on asking for a number. You could amend the program to end
once the 2 is entered by replacing line 30 with:

```
30 IF N=2 THEN END
40 GOTO 10
```

The following lines achieve the same result:

```
30 IF N <> 2 THEN GOTO 10
40 END
```

Thus when N does equal 2, line 30 is ignored and the program
reaches the END statement at line 40.
     The following slightly shorter form is allowable and convenient:

```
30 IF N <> 2 THEN 10
```

Quite complex expressions may be involved. They can appear on
the left as well as the right of the comparison. For instance the
following is a valid comparison. The computer works out the
expression on both sides of the <> before performing the comparison.
Appropriate branching then takes place.

```
1050 IF X*(X^2+Y) <> Y^4+6 THEN 210
```

String variables may also appear in conditional branch
statements. Each of the following is allowable:

```
20 IF answer$="YES" THEN 300
```

and   33 IF ans$=A$ THEN 200

and   56 IF name1$ < name2$ THEN 150

The last example causes a sort into alphabetical order with, for example, JOHNSON coming before JONES. This is because the computer can not only put numbers in ascending order and letters in alphabetical order, but can put in order a mixture of numbers and letters, both upper- and lower-case. It treats numbers before letters and upper-case before lower-case. This is represented in the following way:

0<1<2 . . . <9 . . . <A<B<C<D . . . <Z . . . <a<b<c . . . <z

Almost any practically useful program will contain an IF . . THEN statement. As an illustration of its wide-ranging use, consider a program for a cash register to add up a large number of entries and provide a running total, printed on the screen. We will allow the program to be reset ready for a new transaction by entering 0 for the cost of the current item. The following program lines are suitable:

```
10 total = 0
20 PRINT "Total so far = £";total
30 INPUT "cost of next item "cost
40 IF cost = 0 THEN 10
50 total = total + cost
60 GOTO 20
```

Line 10 sets the value of total to 0. The next line prints out the current total which starts with 0. Once an amount has been entered as a result of the INPUT statement in line 30, a comparison is made to see if its value is 0. Provided the value is not 0, it is added to the current value of total in the line following the IF statement. Resetting of the total back to zero happens when the IF statement detects a zero cost. This results in a jump to the first line of the program.

4.5 Activities

----

i. Without running the following simple program, can you see that it will only continue to run provided the correct response is entered?

```
10 INPUT "Shall I continue",A$
20 IF A$="YES" GOTO 10
30 PRINT "OK then I'll stop"
40 END
```

As a check, enter the program and run it.

ii. Try just pressing the return key in response to the question 'Shall I continue?'. Do you understand why the program stops? (See section 4.17.)

iii. Enter the following program:

```
10 INPUT "Type a number"X
20 PRINT "The number was ";
30 IF X<5 THEN PRINT "<5"
40 IF X>=5 THEN PRINT ">=5"
50 GOTO 10
60 END
```

Study this program to make sure you understand how it operates. Then run it. Can you see other ways of writing a program to give the same results? If so, try writing one, run it and correct any lines in error until it runs correctly. If you feel like a challenge, see how many different versions of the program you could write to give the same results. If you accept this challenge you will quickly see that your programs vary in length and that some are easier to understand than others. Do you consider clarity or brevity to be most important in your own programming?

iv. Enter and run the cash register program of the previous section. Can you suggest modifications to check and question possible negative values? Add a section to keep a total for the day which can be printed out. (See section 4.17 for a discussion on this.)

v. Write a program to accept the entry of a list of numbers so that, when zero is entered, it prints up both the smallest and the largest in the list. (See section 4.17.)

4.6 Grouping conditional statements

It is often necessary to test more than one condition at a time. For example in a cash register program you might want to give a discount on items costing between £20 and £30. In this case you would want the program to jump to the discount section if the cost was greater than £20 and less than £30. BASIC provides the 'logical operators' AND and OR for such occasions. They are used much as in ordinary speech. By way of illustration, we give two alternative ways of doing the same thing, first with two separate lines and then with only one and a logical operator.

Either:
```
35 IF cost <= 20 THEN 100
36 IF cost >= 30 THEN 100
```
Or:
```
35 IF cost<=20 OR cost>=30 THEN 100
```

Each of the comparisons can be as complex as you choose, as

long as the entire statement goes on a single line of up to 240 characters.
    The test for special treatment for numbers greater than 20 and less than 30 may be performed using the AND operator:

        125 IF cost>20 AND cost<30 THEN 400

For numbers between 20 and 30, line 125 causes a branch to line 400 for special treatment, while the normal program follows after line 125.
    Any number of logical operators may be written on the same line with brackets showing priority. For example the following line arranges for Z to be given the value of Y^2 if X=A and Y=B, or if X=3 and Y=4:

        210 IF (X=A AND Y=B) OR (X=3 AND Y=4) THEN Z=Y^2

4.7 The IF . . THEN . . ELSE statement

This statement is a natural extension to the IF statement. If the IF condition is not satisfied, whatever follows the ELSE is executed. For example:

        40 IF answer=2 THEN PRINT "Correct" ELSE PRINT
            "Wrong"

This arranges for an appropriate message to be printed irrespective of whether or not the condition is satisfied: the message is "Correct" if the answer is 2 or "Wrong" if the answer is not 2.

4.8 Multistatement lines

Whatever follows THEN and ELSE may need to be the equivalent of a mini program in its own right. The version of BBC BASIC available early in 1982 does not allow you to put these mini programs on multiple lines after THEN and ELSE. You can get round the problem, within the limitations of the maximum line length, by using what are known as multistatement lines. A multistatement line is one which contains more than one statement on a single line, and is allowable as long as there is a marker to indicate where one statement finishes and the next begins. A colon serves this purpose. By way of illustration, the following shows how the cash register program can be reduced to just two lines:

        10 total = 0
        20 PRINT"Total so far =£";total : INPUT"cost of next item
            "cost : IF cost = 0 THEN 10 ELSE total = total
            + cost : GOTO 20

Programs with such long lines cannot fit into the width of the screen and, as you know, the computer automatically spills them over onto the next screen line. When entering such long lines of program you should take care to press the return key only when you reach the end of the program line and not when you reach the edge of the screen.

Although there will be times when you are forced to use multistatement lines, especially with the IF . . THEN . . ELSE construction, we do not in general recommend them as they can make programs difficult to read.

4.9 Activities

---

i. The previous activities involved a program which could print a message to indicate whether or not an entered number was less than five. Try to rewrite it using an IF . . THEN . . ELSE statement. Use multistatement lines if necessary. (We suggest one possible program in section 4.17.)

ii. Enter your program and see if it runs.

4.10 The ON . . GOTO statement

You will inevitably come across situations where you will want to jump to one of a number of lines according to certain conditions. There is an operation, called ON . . GOTO, which allows a jump to one of a number of lines depending on the value of a variable. An example of an ON . . GOTO statement is:

100 ON X GOTO 100,200,300,105,500

This causes a branch to

line 100 if X=1
line 200 if X=2
line 300 if X=3
line 105 if X=4
line 500 if X=5
and causes an error message if X<1 or X>5

A feature of the BBC BASIC is that ELSE can be used to cause an alternative action if the variable in the ON . . GOTO statement is not within the required range for the line numbers supplied, i.e. 1 to 5 in the above example. The following is an example of ELSE with ON . . GOTO. It computes where to jump for a value of X from 1 to 4, and for any other value prints up the message and stops:

    50 ON X GOTO 10,400,80,200 ELSE PRINT"Value out of
       range" : END

4.11 Activities

---

i. Enter and run the following program which illustrates the action of an ON . . GOTO statement.

```
 10 PRINT"Numbering the days of the week 1 to 7"
 20 INPUT"enter today's number "N
 30 IF N<1 OR N>7 THEN 10
 40 PRINT"Yes it's ";
 50 ON N GOTO 60,70,80,90,100,110,120
 60 PRINT"Sunday"    : GOTO 20
 70 PRINT"Monday"    : GOTO 20
 80 PRINT"Tuesday"   : GOTO 20
 90 PRINT"Wednesday" : GOTO 20
100 PRINT"Thursday"  : GOTO 20
110 PRINT"Friday"    : GOTO 20
120 PRINT"Saturday"  : GOTO 20
130 END
```

4.12 The STOP and END statements

There are two instructions to cease execution of a program: STOP and END.

As you know, END indicates the end of a program. However, some of the previous example programs would have been simpler if they had ended with lines of the form:

    100 INPUT "Do you wish to try another value",ans$
    110 IF ans$="YES" THEN 10 ELSE END

A line like 110 need not be the last line of a program. END, used in this way, may appear a number of times throughout programs.

A STOP statement interrupts and stops a program while it is running and also causes a message stating the line number at which execution ceased. This can be useful when 'debugging' programs - i.e. identifying and remedying faults. You can restart the program if you know the number of the following line. If it is say 450, then enter GOTO 450. This statement is then executed as an immediate action and causes the program to restart from line 450 with all variables holding their current values.

    While a program is interrupted, any of the variable values can be examined - which is very useful for debugging. You merely enter PRINT Var, where Var is the name of the variable you wish to examine. You can change the values of variables at this stage by means of a LET statement. No line number is required. Thus to debug your program, insert a STOP statement at each critical stage. Then every time the program stops execution, you will know the line number reached from the message printed on the screen. Examine the value of all the variables to see if they are as you would expect at that stage of the program. If everything is in order, then continue execution using GOTO.

4.13 The REM statement

You will now be writing some quite complex programs and the variety of ways of writing them will become more difficult to remember. This is where the REM statement is useful. It provides a way of keeping notes within a program to remind you why you wrote it as you did or to point out anything else that you might want to remember. You merely have to begin the line by typing REM, after which you may type in anything you like. The computer ignores it, but stores it so that you can look at it again by listing. The following are examples of REM statements:

```
10 REM This is a section of program which does
20 REM nothing at all. It is advisable to keep
30 REM plenty of notes of how you designed
40 REM your favourite program. We
50 REM assure you that you will soon forget.
```

    Empty REM statements are useful in long programs as visual markers between sections. The positions of such short three letter lines are obvious at a glance and the computer does not act on them. We shall illustrate such use later.

4.14 Activities

----

i. You may like to try running the following program which allows you to work out your United Kingdom income tax for the year and compare it with your tax returns. It uses very simple calculations with just two comparisons, and requires you to supply your total taxable income for the year, your personal allowances and how the tax rate changes with income.

When it asks for personal allowances, you must enter a figure which includes all allowances allowed against pay. The program could be

extended to ask for all possible variations but this refinement is
omitted for simplicity.

For how the tax rate changes with income, you may use the following
fictitious data:

TAX RATE   FROM   TO

30%	1	11249
35%	11250	13249
40%	13250	15000
etc.		

```
10 REM A tax calculation program
20 INPUT"Enter total taxable income "income
30 INPUT"Enter total personal allowances "allowances
40 income_left = income - allowances :tax=0
50 IF income_left<0 THEN 200
60 INPUT"Enter lowest tax rate%"tax_rate
70 bottom_range=0
80 PRINT"Enter the income range for which"
90 PRINT"this tax rate applies ";bottom_range;" to "
100 INPUT top_range
110 range = top_range - bottom_range + 1
120 REM Now calculate the tax payable at this rate after
130 REM first finding on how much income this tax is
    payable
140 IF range>income_left THEN tax=tax + income_left
    *tax_rate/100 : GOTO 200
150 tax = tax + range*tax_rate/100
160 income_left = income_left - range
170 bottom_range = top_range + 1
180 INPUT"Enter next tax rate% "tax_rate
190 GOTO 80
200 PRINT "Taxable income =£";income
210 PRINT "Personal allowances =£";allowances
220 PRINT "tax payable =£";tax
230 PRINT "Nett Income =£";income - tax
240 END
```

The program works out how much tax is payable in each band and
prints out the total.

4.15 Some points to think about

a.   What can halt the execution of a program?
b.   When using an ON . . GOTO statement is there any limit to

the number of possible line numbers, their order or their values?

c. What happens if the value between ON and GOTO is too large?

d. What limits the complexity of the IF . . THEN . . ELSE statement?

e. How do you feel about writing your programs to:

-   occupy as few lines as possible?
-   run quickly?
-   use clever tricks?
-   be easy to read?

4.16 Discussion on the points to think about

a. A program can cease executing if:
-   it has come across an erroneous line
-   it has run out of program to execute
-   it has encountered an END or STOP statement
-   the escape key has been pressed.

b. ON . . GOTO statements must be stored on one program line. The line numbers can be in any order and have any legal line number values between 0 and 32767.

c. If the value between ON and GOTO is either negative, zero or too large, an error message is issued and execution of the program stops. ON . . GOTO may be followed by ELSE, in which case this part will be executed if the ON . . GOTO part is out of range.

d. The main limitations are due to having to keep this statement to one line. However, any complex arithmetic conditions can frequently be simplified in previous program lines.

e. We have no answers here. Everyone must develop their own style of programming. While on the subject of programming style, we would like to point out that you should keep notes as prompts in the form of REM statements.

4.17 Discussion of activities

4.2 iii. If you start a program by entering GOTO 10 instead of RUN, the variables are not reset to zero. Thus a program can be reexecuted from any line you like. You can even alter the value of a variable by entering the new value using an immediate action. For instance entering just X = 26 gives the variable X the value 26. If you then start the program by using GOTO 30, X retains the value 26. RUN always starts the program from the beginning and with variables reset. The BBC Microcomputer is slightly unusual in that it does not accept RUN XX where XX is a line number.

4.5 ii. Just pressing the return key results in the value 0 or an
empty string - as appropriate - being given to the variable in the
INPUT statement.

4.5 iv. To check for negative values and question them requires some
lines of the form:

```
35 IF cost >= 0 THEN 40
36 INPUT "Do you mean negative",A$
38 IF A$ <> "YES" THEN 30
```

To keep a total for the day, the following few lines will do in
addition to lines 35 and 38 above:

```
37 IF A$ = "DAY" THEN 100
60 day = day + cost
70 GOTO 20
100 PRINT' "Total for the day is £";day
110 END
```

4.5 v. The following program accepts a continuous stream of numbers
until zero is entered. The first is taken as both the maximum and the
minimum value. Thereafter the maximum and minimum is adjusted
according to the size of the most recent number entered.

```
10 INPUT"Enter your number "num
20 min = num
30 max = num
40 INPUT"Enter your number, 0=end "num
50 IF num = 0 THEN 100
60 IF num < min THEN min = num
70 IF num > max THEN max = num
80 GOTO 40
100 PRINT "Min number = ";min;" max = ";max
110 END
```

4.9 i. The following is just one of what must be many ways of
writing a program to take a number using an INPUT statement and
then saying whether it is less than 5:

```
10 INPUT "Enter a number "num
20 PRINT "That number was ";
30 IF num < 5 THEN PRINT"<5" ELSE PRINT">=5"
40 GOTO 10
50 END
```

Stepping through loops

5 Loops

5.0 Introduction

There are many occasions when a process has to be repeated a number of times. 'Loop' structures facilitate this.

5.1 The FOR . . NEXT loop

The FOR . . NEXT construction is the simplest way of arranging for a group of lines to be repeated within a program. The instruction is given in terms of what is called the 'loop variable'. We shall explain by means of the following example in which the loop variable V has a starting value of 1. Line 10 instructs that the program be repeated twelve times. Lines 20 to 40 are executed normally. At line 50, NEXT V causes the loop to begin again with V increased by one. The program ceases to run when V goes beyond 12.

```
10 FOR V = 1 TO 12
20 . . .
30 . . .
40 . . .
50 NEXT V
```

The loop variable need not be increased by one every time the loop is repeated. By including a STEP instruction, it can be increased by whatever increment you choose. For example, the following line instructs that the loop variable should start at 1, and go up with a 'loop increment' of 0.3. The program finishes when the loop has been repeated 24 times.

```
10 FOR V = 1 TO 8 STEP 0.3
```

We can illustrate the use of the FOR . . NEXT construction by considering a program to list the squares of the numbers from 1 to 10. We already know how IF and GOTO statements could do this. As the following example shows, the computer repeatedly runs through the lines of program between 10 and 50 until the value of N reaches 11, whereupon the looping finishes and any program lines beyond 50 are executed:

```
10 N=1
20 square = N*N
30 PRINT N;" squared= ";square
40 N=N+1
50 IF N <= 10 GOTO 20
```

Alternatively, using the FOR . . NEXT construction:

```
10 FOR num = 1 TO 10
20    square = num*num
30    PRINT num;" squared = ";square
40 NEXT num
```

Line 10 sets up the loop variable num as a counter for the number of times the lines 20 and 30 are to be executed. When line 10 is executed, num is given the value 1. Lines 20 and 30 are executed in the normal manner and line 40 causes the loop variable num to be incremented by 1. The new value of num is then tested to see if it has passed the value 10. If it has, the loop finishes. If not, the loop is repeated again.

You may have noticed that we inset the statements on lines 20 and 30. This was to demonstrate the structure of the program. Although the practice is entirely optional, we recommend it as it facilitates program checking and debugging.

Although it is usual to think of the loop variable as increasing, it can be made to decrease by assigning a negative value to the loop increment. This may be illustrated by the following alternative line 10 in the program for giving the squares of numbers:

```
10 FOR num = 10 TO 1 STEP -1
```

The squares of fractional numbers from, say, 8 to 6 in steps of 0.2 could be obtained using yet another version of line 10:

```
10 FOR num = 8 TO 6 STEP -0.2
```

FOR . . NEXT loops are widely used in programming. A further illustration is a program to print a table of temperature conversions from the Fahrenheit scale to the Centigrade scale using the following conversion formula:

$$\text{Centigrade temp} = (\text{Fahrenheit temp} - 32)*5/9$$

The program allows you to print the conversion table over whatever range you choose:

```
10 REM A conversion from Fahrenheit
20 REM temperatures to Centigrade.
30 INPUT"Enter start and finish temperature",start,end
40 inc = 1
50 IF start > end THEN inc = -1
60 FOR Ftemp = start TO end STEP inc
70 PRINT;Ftemp;" degrees F = ";(Ftemp-32)*5/9;" degrees
   C"
80 NEXT Ftemp
90 END
```

5.2 Activities

----

i. Enter and run the two forms of the number squaring program of the last section. Do both work as you expect?

ii. Try the following alternative:

```
10 FOR num = 1 TO 10
20    square = num * num
30    PRINT num;" squared = ";square
44    num = num-1
40 NEXT num
```

Can you see what is happening? Although the program does not execute as the previous version, why is there no error message? (This is discussed in section 5.12.)

iii. Enter the following simple program which illustrates the progress of a FOR . . NEXT loop and, in particular, the value of the loop variable on exit from the loop. Before running it, try to work out the form of the printout. Run the program and see if you are right.

```
10 FOR I = 1 TO 5
20    PRINT;I;
30 NEXT I
40 PRINT I
50 END
```

iv. Try using a FOR . . NEXT construction to write a program to add all the numbers from 1 to 10. (We give some hints and comments in section 5.12.) Run the program. Does it give the answer 55?

v. Try entering and running the temperature conversion program of the previous section. Does it work as you expect?

vi. Can you think of other conversions that you might like a program to provide?

5.3 Traps for the unwary

As you acquire more powerful statements, you have to be more careful in using them - because, as you saw in the previous activities, it is quite possible for the computer to run a program but produce no useful results. Nevertheless, although the FOR . . NEXT loop does open up possibilities of trouble, these are easily avoided if you are ready for them.

For example, as illustrated in the previous activities, changing the loop variable inside a loop is something to avoid. Although it does not necessarily cause any error, you will probably find difficulty in foreseeing all its effects, particularly in a long program - and a program which produces errors just some of the time can be more troublesome than one which always gives them.

Branching into a loop by means of a GOTO is also to be avoided. If you did it, it would almost certainly cause havoc because the loop variable would take on an unpredictable value. Branching out of a loop is allowable, but is best not done too often as it leaves the loop still set up.

5.4 REPEAT . . UNTIL loops

The REPEAT . . UNTIL loop is another way of arranging for a group of lines to be repeated within a program. Whereas a FOR . . NEXT loop causes the subsection to repeat until a specified number of repetitions have been completed, a REPEAT . . UNTIL loop continues until a specified condition is met, i.e. the group of lines between REPEAT and UNTIL is executed until the condition written in the UNTIL statement occurs.

By way of illustration, the following program asks for someone to enter the cost of a list of items which it then adds up. The list can be of any length. It ends only when someone enters 0. The program then prints out the sum of the amounts:

```
10 total = 0
20 REPEAT
30    INPUT "Item cost (end=0)",cost
40    total = total + cost
50 UNTIL cost = 0
60 PRINT "The total =";total
70 END
```

The group of lines to be repeated is clearly identifiable by the bounding REPEAT and UNTIL. Inset lines make the structure even clearer in a fashion that cannot be achieved with IF . . GOTO.

Incidentally line 50 is equivalent to:

```
50 IF cost <> 0 GOTO 30.
```

5.5 Activities

---

i. Use a REPEAT . . UNTIL construction to write a program to print out numbers from 1 to 10 together with their squares. Then try your program out on the computer and correct any errors. If you are unable to work out a program of your own, use the one in section 5.12. It may look very different from yours, but any program is valid if it gives the right answers in all circumstances.

ii. Factorial N, written N!, is a mathematical and engineering term which is the product of all the integers from 1 to N. N! may be calculated from the following formula:

$$N! = N*(N-1)*(N-2)*(N-3)*. . . *4*3*2*1$$

Try writing a program to calculate N! for any number from 1 to 33. As a hint, the calculation could start with:

```
factN = 1
. . . . .
. . . . .
```

and have repetition of the lines:

```
factN = factN*N%
N% = N% - 1
```

(Further hints are in section 5.12.)

5.6 Loops within loops

As an introduction to loops within loops, we will develop a program to print out the following pattern of six lines of crosses, each line with a number of crosses equal to one more than the line number:

```
XX
XXX
XXXX
XXXXX
XXXXXX
XXXXXXX
```

A program to print, say, three crosses on a single line would be as follows, the three being defined by the number of times the loop is processed:

```
10 L = 3
20 FOR N = 1 TO L
30    PRINT "X";
40 NEXT N
50 PRINT
```

Printing six lines with successive numbers of crosses could be achieved by repeating the above program lines with L increasing successively from 2 to 7. This can be accomplished with a FOR . . NEXT loop as shown in the following program:

```
10 FOR L = 2 TO 7
20    FOR N = 1 TO L
30       PRINT "X";
40    NEXT N
50    PRINT
```

60 NEXT L

Here we have an outer loop with loop variable L and another inner loop with loop variable N. The value of the outer loop sets the range of values in the inner one.

There can be many inner loops within an outer loop. The process is called 'nesting'. Any type of loop can be nested within or outside any other, although you will probably find fewer occasions when you want to nest REPEAT . . UNTIL loops.

It is very important that a loop should be either completely within another or completely outside it. In the following schematic diagram loop B is entirely within loop A, and is allowable:

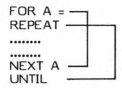

```
FOR A =
FOR B =
.......
.......
NEXT B
NEXT A
```

The following schematic diagram represents overlapping loops which are in error:

```
FOR A =
REPEAT
........
........
NEXT A
UNTIL
```

The BBC Microcomputer allows the name of the loop variable - A in this case - to be missed off from the NEXT statement. However, we do not recommend the practice because, if your program erroneously contains overlapped loops, no error message warns you. The program might run, but possibly erroneously.

5.7 Activities

Try writing a program to print the times tables up to ten for numbers from 2 to 10. As a hint, this is most conveniently achieved by a loop within a loop. (Further hints and comments are provided in section 5.12.)

5.8 Multistatement lines

You will remember that it is allowable and sometimes very convenient to put more than one statement on a line and that BASIC requires a colon to mark off where one statement finishes and the next begins.

One instance of the use of a multistatement line is for a FOR . . NEXT loop, inserted into a program to produce a time delay. The one action of delay can be completed on one line, as shown in the following program line. With the BBC Microcomputer this causes a pause of about one second:

```
100 FOR I=1 TO 1400: NEXT I
```

Although the FOR . . NEXT loop has nothing inside it, it is still started, and the loop variable is incremented in steps. Although the time on each loop is small, there is not much limit on the number of times you can force the computer to execute it, and hence on how long the delays are. The time delay can be adjusted by varying the start and finish value of the loop variable. When the loop eventually finishes, the next program line is executed.

The following crude program uses the technique to imitate a digital clock:

```
 10 INPUT"Type time as HOUR,MIN,SEC "hour,min,sec
 20 PRINT "Time is ";hour;"  ";min;" and";sec;
    " secs"
 30 delay=1329
 40 sec=sec+1:IF sec=60 THEN sec=0 ELSE 100
 50 delay=1324
 60 min=min+1:IF min=60 THEN min=0 ELSE 100
 70 delay=1320
 80 hour=hour+1: IF hour=24 THEN hour=0 ELSE 100
 90 delay=1316
100 FOR del=0 TO delay: NEXT del
110 GOTO 20
```

The program successively reduces the value of delay to allow for the time the preceding IF statements take to process. The program ignores the ELSE part if the first part of the IF condition is satisfied. In this case the next line to be executed is the line that follows.

5.9 Activities

----

i. The following program illustrates a REPEAT . . UNTIL loop. It calculates the mortgage still owing as the years progress, dependent on the interest paid and the monthly repayments. Examine the listing, and when you understand the program, try running it:

```
10 REM mortgage calculation.
20 PRINT"Enter capital, monthly repayment, interest rate%"
30 INPUT capital,repayment,interest
40 REPEAT
50    year = year + 1
60    PRINT"year ";year;", Capital ";capital
70    capital=capital+capital*interest/100-12*repayment
80 UNTIL capital<0
90 END
```

The printout of successive lines from such programs may be too rapid to read. Can you suggest and try out two ways of slowing it down? (See section 5.17.)

5.10 Points to think about

a. Is the following grouping of FOR . . NEXT loops allowable?

```
            FOR A= . . 1 TO 10
            FOR B= . . 1 TO 10
            . . . . .
            . . . . .
            NEXT B
            FOR J= . . 1 TO 10
            . . . . .
            NEXT J
            NEXT A
            FOR Z= . . 1 TO 10
            . . . . .
            NEXT Z
```

b. Which of the following variable types are suitable for loop variables:

      integer, numerical, string?

c. What is the value of K after the following loop has been completed?

```
            FOR K = 3 TO 5 STEP 0.2
            NEXT K
```

d. What is the value of G after the following loop has completed?

```
            G = 100
            REPEAT
            G = G + 2
```

UNTIL G > 139

5.11 Discussion on the points to think about

a. The loops are all allowably nested. If you draw a line from each FOR to the corresponding NEXT, none cross. This is a good test of whether loops are correctly nested, and is shown below.

```
FOR A= ──────┐
FOR B= ──┐   │
  . . .   │  │
  . . .   │  │
NEXT B ──┘   │
FOR J= ──┐   │
  . . .   │  │
NEXT J ──┘   │
NEXT A ──────┘
FOR Z= ──┐
  . . .   │
NEXT Z ──┘
```

b. The loop variable in a FOR . . NEXT loop may be of any type other than string. The integer variable is preferable.
c. 5.2.
d. 140.

5.12 Discussion of activities

5.2 ii. In the suggested program a new line has been inserted which varies the value of the loop variable inside the loop. Consequently the loop variable is reset to its starting value each time this line is executed. The result is a loop which executes for ever. It is, from a programming point of view, rather dangerous to alter the loop variable inside a loop. You may use a loop variable at any stage, but it is best not to alter it.

5.2 iv. The following is an example of a program to add all the numbers from 1 to 10 using a FOR . . NEXT loop:

```
10 REM Program to add all numbers from 1 to 10
20 sum = 0
30 FOR N% = 1 TO 10
40    sum = sum + N%
50 NEXT N%
60 PRINT sum
70 END
```

5.5 i. The following program prints out squares of numbers from 1 to 10:

```
10 REM Print the squares from 1 to 10
20 number = 1
30 REPEAT
30   PRINT"Number ";number;" squared = ";number*number
40   number = number + 1
50 UNTIL number>10
60 END
```

5.5 ii. The program could start by asking for a number. As this number must be an integer, we will use the integer variable N%. Then provided the number is in the correct range, we could continue with the line:

```
70 fact = 1
```

Then could follow a repetition of the two lines:

```
90 fact = fact*N%
100 N% = N% - 1
```

These could be repeated until the last used value of N% is 1. We suggest some of the key program lines could be:

```
20 INPUT"Enter a number "N%
```

```
     put here some lines to check
     for the correct range of N%
```

```
60 PRINT N%;" factorial = ";
70 fact = 1
```

```
     start of loop
```

```
90 fact = fact*N%
100 N%=N%-1
```

```
     end of loop
```

```
120 PRINT fact
130 GOTO 20
```

A complete program is as follows:

```
10 REM Factorial printing program
20 INPUT"Enter a number "N%
30 IF N% <34 AND N% > 0 THEN 60
40 PRINT"Factorial out of range"
50 GOTO 20
60 PRINT N%;" factorial = ";
70 fact = 1
```

```
 80 REPEAT
 90    fact = fact*N%
100    N%=N%-1
110 UNTIL N%<=1
120 PRINT fact
130 GOTO 10
140 END
```

Note that this program will not accept values out of the range 1 to 33. This keeps the answer within the size of variables that the computer can handle. The integer variable in the INPUT statement forces the use of only integer values by the program.

You may also have thought of the following line which will work out the value of factorial N%:

```
80 FOR J%=1 TO N% :fact = fact*J% : NEXT J%
```

5.7 A times table program can be written using a double FOR . . NEXT loop as shown below. The outer loop dictates which times table is the current one, while the inner loop prints it.

```
10 REM times table printing program
20 FOR J = 2 TO 10
30    FOR K = 1 TO 10
40       PRINT J;" times ";K;" = ";J*K
50    NEXT K
60 NEXT J
70 END
```

5.9 i. The rate at which programs print up information can be conveniently slowed down in two ways. The first is to include a time delay FOR . . NEXT loop, probably written on one line. The second is with an INPUT statement to ask if the user is ready for more information.

Filing programs

6 Program management

6.0 Introduction

Computer programs are no use without data to work on. There are various ways in which data can be fed into a program and, as the amount increases, it becomes more important to have it in some permanent form.

The first part of this chapter considers storing data within a program and storing programs on tape. The second half considers editing programs and any data stored within them. Editing is a feature which probably varies more than any other from computer to computer. Some are delightfully easy to edit on, while others have only very crude editing facilities. The BBC Microcomputer is fairly good in this respect, which we shall exploit to the full.

6.1 The DATA statement

It may sometimes be rather lengthy to supply programs with data using LET and INPUT statements. This is particularly true with large amounts of data, and where the data is the same each time the program is run.

By way of illustration, consider a program to test a person's French by simply printing an English word and asking for the French equivalent. The program could test the response against a store of answers and issue a message of congratulation or otherwise. With just LET and INPUT statements for handling the data, the program might be as follows:

```
100 INPUT"What is the French for A HORSE",ANS$
110 IF ANS$ <> "UN CHEVAL" then 100
120 PRINT "correct"
130 INPUT"What is the French for A PIG",ANS$
140 . . .
```

Although the program would be simple to write, it would be very long and clumsy. It would require many more lines than the number of words in the test vocabulary and, to be of much use, the stored vocabulary and therefore the length of the program would have to be considerable. There would also be the problem that any changes in the list of test words would require major changes to the program.

In such situations the DATA statement is very useful indeed because it allows data to be stored in a compact form within a program. As many numerical and string values as you choose can be stored together in any order on the same line. The number is limited only by the line length. The pieces of data must be written as a list with each item separated from the next by a comma. For example the numbers 1001 and 215, together with the string "UN CHEVAL" may be stored as follows:

```
1000 DATA 1001,215,"UN CHEVAL"
```

Any number of lines of DATA statement can be included in a program and they may be inserted anywhere. It is a good policy, however, to keep them all together at the end of the program so that the earlier line numbers are not affected if the number of DATA statements has to be changed.

The computer retrieves data from DATA statements in response to a statement called READ. Whereas the INPUT statement requires the data to be entered by the person running the program, the READ statement causes the computer to take it directly from the DATA statements.

You will now see how DATA statements can cope with the problem of testing a person's French spelling. The equivalent English and French words can be stored as a list, in pairs. The following would be one version of a suitable program:

```
  10 PRINT"This is a program to test your knowledge
     of French"
  20 PRINT"It will print an English word(s) on the
     screen and"
  30 PRINT"then wait for you to type the French.
     Follow"
  40 PRINT"each French equivalent by pressing the
     'return' key"
  50 READ eng$,fr$
  60 PRINT"What is the French for ";eng$;
  70 INPUT ans$
  80 IF ans$ <> fr$ THEN PRINT"No" : GOTO 60
  90 PRINT "correct"
 100 GOTO 50
1000 DATA "A KEY","UNE   CLEF","A KNIFE","UN
     COUTEAU"
1010 DATA "A DRAWING","UN DESSIN"
```

This program starts by printing the messages in lines 10 to 40. Line 50 contains the READ statement and has two string variables - although a READ statement could just as well contain any number of variable names separated by commas. As soon as the computer reaches a READ statement, it goes to the first DATA statement and considers all the string or numerical values - within both it and the following DATA statements - as one long list to work through. For each variable name in the READ statement, it takes the next value in the list and gives that value to the variable. It keeps a record of how far it has gone down this list so that each time a new variable appears in a READ statement the next value in the list is used. The program continues until no more values are available in the DATA statements. If any further READ statements are encountered, the computer issues an error message saying that it is out of data.

In a READ statement, just as in an INPUT statement, it is important for a numerical value to be given to a numerical variable and a string to be given to a string variable. If a numerical value is given to a string variable, no computers recognize the error. If a program tries to read a string where a numerical value is required, many computers issue an error message. The BBC Microcomputer issues no such message. So you should be careful to avoid this kind of programming error.

6.2 RESTORE

There will be times when you would like to alter the starting point from which the computer reads values from DATA statements. The RESTORE statement allows this. For example RESTORE N forces the program to read data values starting from the DATA statement in line N, where N can be a line number or an expression which gives the line number.

We shall explain by imagining the following simple language-translation program with DATA lines containing both French and German test words. The person taking the test is asked which language he wants to be tested on, whereupon a RESTORE statement allows the data to be read from the appropriate vocabulary.

```
10 PRINT"A vocabulary test in French or German"
20 INPUT"Type 1 for French and 2 for German"N
30 IF N=1 THEN RESTORE 1000
40 IF N=2 THEN RESTORE 2000
50 . . . .
60 . . . .

1000 DATA "A HOUSE","UNE MAISON","A GARDEN","UN
     JARDIN"
1010 DATA . . . .

2000 DATA "A TABLE","EIN TISCH","A PENCIL","EIN
     BLEISTIFT"
2010 DATA . . . .
```

In this simple form, the program finishes with an error message due to running out of data. This is not a very elegant way of ending a program. In the following activities you are asked to make suggestions about how to prevent it.

6.3 Activities

----

i. Enter and run either language-test program, substituting a test topic of your own.

ii. Can you modify the language-test program so as to show the translation if someone enters R, as a shortened form for REVEAL THE ANSWER? (See section 6.13.)

iii. Suggest two ways in which you could modify the program so that, when it runs out of data, it ends at an end statement rather than with an error message. (See section 6.13.)

iv. Can you modify the program so as to keep a note of how many times the user gets the correct answer first time? You could then add some program lines that print up his score upon completion. (See section 6.13.)

_____

6.4 Saving programs on tape

Without the facility to save programs, computers would be of very little use. The BBC Microcomputer can save programs onto either cassette tapes or floppy discs. We will assume that you will be using cassette tapes and that you have a cassette recorder connected as instructed in the manual.

Most microcomputers are a little temperamental in their relationship with the cassette recorder. So it is very important to use good quality tape. Cheap tapes can have small gaps in the recording medium which, although giving barely perceptible effects on sound reproduction, can play havoc with recorded computer programs. The quality of the tape recorder seems far less critical, as long as it can give out a strong - and preferably adjustable - signal. A model with a mechanically adjustable recording level is better than one with an automatic recording level. This is because the signal from the computer is of constant level, whereas a normal recording of speech shows very considerable changes of volume. The optimum setting of the recording level from a computer is therefore very much higher than for speech as it need include no allowance for variations.

To save a program on cassette tape, wind the tape forwards past the leader (which is usually a different colour). Then enter the following (where ProgramX can be any name you choose as long as it does not contain spaces and is of less than eleven characters):

        SAVE "ProgramX"

Then turn the tape recorder on in the record mode and press the return key.

The computer will accept no more commands until the program has finished recording. Obviously, the longer the program, the longer it will take to save.

To check that your program has recorded successfully, enter:

        *CAT

Now wind the tape back to the start and set the tape recorder to play. The computer will print up the name of each program it finds on the tape. If it finds an error, it will print a message such as:

        Data?
        Rewind tape

To retrieve a program from tape, rewind the tape, and enter the following, where ProgramX is the name of the program required from your tape:

LOAD "ProgramX"

Next set the tape recorder to 'play'. While the computer searches, it prints up the names of all the programs on the tape, as it comes to them. It otherwise ignores them. Once it finds the specified program, it reads in a copy from the tape to its memory, just as if you had typed it in. If it cannot find the name, it carries on trying until it reaches the end of the tape. You can get back into the command mode by pressing the escape key.

6.5 A short form for statements

The BBC Microcomputer has a facility whereby you may enter a short form for statements. Examples include P. for PRINT and RU. for RUN. All statements can be reduced in this way while typing in a program. The computer translates them into their usual form when it stores the line in memory. This means that, despite having used the shortened form of a statement when entering a program, it gets listed out in the usual expanded form on all listings. For example:

1 RU. L. P. RENU.

is listed as:

1 RUN LIST PRINT RENUMBER

We will not use any of the abbreviated forms in this book as they tend to make the programs less readable.

6.6 Activities

_____

i. Enter the program lines:

1 A. B. C. D.
2 E. F. G. H.

Then list the program by entering L.

ii. Make a guess at the abbreviated form for each of the statements you have met so far. Enter lines with these abbreviations and then list the program to see if your guess was correct.

_____

6.7 Editing program lines

So far you have retyped a program line to correct any error in it. A more satisfactory method is just to correct the part of the line concerned, leaving the rest unchanged. This procedure is not only quicker, but it also introduces fewer secondary typing errors.

The editing on the BBC Microcomputer allows you to keep as much of the faulty line as you wish by inserting or deleting parts. It requires the 'copy' key which is on the lower right-hand side of the keyboard and the 'cursor-control' keys, of which there are four. They are at the top right-hand side of the keyboard, and move the cursor up, down, to the left and to the right.

To edit a particular line, start by listing the section of program containing that line. Then use the cursor-control keys to bring the cursor to the beginning of the line. Next press the 'copy' key. Each time you do so, the cursor moves one character along the line while at the same time 'copying' the character at the bottom of the screen, where it creates a new program line. When you reach where you want to insert, type the new characters in the normal way; when you reach where you want to delete, use the cursor-control keys to reposition the cursor before continuing to press the copy key. Changes are incorporated into the new line at the bottom of the screen. Only when you press the return key is the editing entered and complete. If you omit to enter, the line remains unchanged.

6.8 Activities

To familiarize yourself with the editing facilities, enter the following program:

```
10 REM A practice program
20 FOR I = 1 to 5
30    PRINT I
40 NEXT I
50 END
```

List and run the program to make sure that you have entered it correctly. Now alter lines 20,30,40 to:

```
20 FOR loop=1 TO 5 STEP .5
30    PRINT loop
40 NEXT loop
```

If you have any difficulties, read the previous section again. Practise with as many variations as you feel necessary.

6.9 Program debugging

You are a very rare person indeed if you can always write programs
without errors. If the computer spots the error and prints up an
error message, you are lucky! Then the debugging is comparatively
simple. The error message tells you the number of the offending line,
and the error will probably be obvious when you examine that line.
Just as often there are the more subtle and potentially more
dangerous errors where the program runs but produces an incorrect
result. An example from everyday life is the bill for £0.0. This is
not a computer error. It is a human, programming error.

Although we cannot give a comprehensive treatise on program
debugging, we will try to give some guidelines on how you can
identify and rectify errors. All program debugging is a matter of
finding where the operation of the program differs from what you had
in mind when writing the program. Once you have found the point of
departure, it is up to you to decide why it occurred and what is the
solution.

You met a common programming error in one of the activities on
branching, where you experienced a program running in an endless
loop. As the loop printed something to the screen, you knew what
was happening. All too frequently, however, you will not get this
indication. It is as if the system is dead. In such situations just
press the escape key. Then the number of the line in operation at
the time is printed up. You can then list the surrounding lines to
see if you can spot the cause.

While the operation of a program is suspended, it is possible to
list any part of it. You may also examine the value held by any
variable. To see the current value of a variable, merely instruct that
it be printed as an immediate action. For example, if num, A$ and C
are the variables whose values you wish to examine, just enter:

PRINT num,A$,C

You can still reexecute a program from the position at which it
stopped by entering GOTO XX where XX is the line number
following the one at which it stopped. The escape key only stops the
computer when it reaches the end of the current line. So no lines
will be left partly complete. You may use this stopping and starting
as often as you like, but it will be difficult to stop every few lines.
The execution of the program is so rapid that it may execute a
hundred lines or so between your entering GOTO XX and pressing
the escape key.

A way to halt execution every few lines is by sprinkling the
program liberally with lines stating STOP. When the program ceases
execution upon encountering STOP, it not only stops running but also
prints the line number where it stopped. It can be restarted at the
following line using GOTO XX as already described. At each stop
you can examine the program listing, decide on the values that
variables should have and then print them out using PRINT as an

immediate action.

TRACE is a facility provided on the BBC Microcomputer and on other better computers. As an immediate action, entering TRACE ON causes the printing of the numbers of all lines as they are executed. As program statements, TRACE ON and TRACE OFF limit the line numbers to be traced. For instance the program:

```
10 C=1
20 P=2
25 TRACE ON
30 FOR J = 1 TO 5
40    C=C+1
50 NEXT J
55 TRACE OFF
60 PRINT P + C
70 END
```

produces the printout:

‹30› ‹40› ‹50› ‹50› ‹50› ‹50› ‹50› ‹55›
        8

Line 50 is traced five times because the FOR . . NEXT loop is for 1 to 5. The single 40 is because the trace is in the order of the execution of the lines by the 'interpreter' which runs the BASIC. For loops it produces this apparently odd effect, but once you are used to this, it still provides a useful indication of what is happening within the program. The 8 is because any normal display printed by the program appears with the trace output.

If you leave the trace on for a long program, the screen quickly gets filled and scrolls up unreadably fast. For rough results you can quickly press the escape key temporarily to stop execution. For a more controlled result, put the trace around only a few program lines at a time, perhaps followed by STOP to allow you to check the values of variables as an immediate action.

6.10 Activities

----

i. The following program illustrates the peculiarities of the trace option. Enter and run it. Examine the listing and see if you can understand the appearance of what is printed on the screen:

```
10 PRINT "Line 10"
20 C = C + 1
30 TRACE ON
40 FOR J = 1 TO 5
50    C = C + 1
```

```
60    PRINT "Line 60",C
70 NEXT J
80 TRACE OFF
90 PRINT "Line 90, C=";C
100 END
```

6.11 Some points to think about

a. Should a program be tested before all of it has been entered
   into the computer?
b. Why might it be preferable to have all DATA statements at the
   end of a program?
c. Can DATA statements be saved on tape?

6.12 Discussion on the points to think about

a. It is often easier to divide a program into sections which can
   be tested and debugged separately. Only when each section is
   shown to function properly, need the next section be entered.
b. If all the DATA statements are at the end of a program, it is
   easier to enter new ones without affecting the rest of the
   program.
c. DATA statements get saved on cassette tape along with the
   rest of a program. If you want, you may of course delete the
   earlier lines of program before saving. Then it is easier to have
   the DATA statements all together as one identifiable block.
   After the DATA statements are retrieved from tape by entering
   LOAD "ProgramX", a program to use the data can be typed in.

6.13 Discussion of activities

6.3 ii. The following multistatement line displays the answer if R is
entered. It also arranges for a move onto the next item in the test.
The program does not keep a check of how many times the user asks
to see the answer or how many times he gets the answer correct
first time.

```
75 IF ans$ = "R" THEN PRINT"French
   for ";eng$;" is "; fr$ : GOTO 50
```

The complete program becomes:

```
10 PRINT"This is a program to test your knowledge
   of French"
```

```
 20 PRINT"It will print an English word(s) on the
    screen and"
 30 PRINT"then wait for you to type the French.
    Follow"
 40 PRINT"each French equivalent by pressing the
    return key"
 50 PRINT "Enter R to see the answer"
 60 READ eng$,fr$
 70 PRINT"What is the French for ";eng$
 80 INPUT ans$
 90 IF ans$ = "R" THEN PRINT"French
    for ";eng$;" is ";fr$" : GOTO 60
100 IF ans$ <> fr$ THEN 70
110 PRINT "correct"
120 GOTO 60
1000 DATA "A KEY","UNE CLEF","A KNIFE,"UN
    COUTEAU"
1010 DATA "A DRAWING","UN DESSIN"
```

6.3 iii. There are two straightforward ways of checking whether a program is about to run out of data. One is to make the first item of data the number of items to follow. This number is then read in and reduced every time data is read. When the remaining number of items of data is zero the program must stop or go onto some other activity.

The following lines inserted in the program achieve this checking.

```
 54 READ Items
 60 Items = Items - 1 : IF Items< 0 THEN END
 65 READ eng$,fr$
1000 DATA 3,"A KEY","UNE CLEF"   etc.
```

A second method is to include a code word at the end of the list of data. Provided this is not likely to be a part of the list, it can be checked for and, when found, the program can be concluded. This method has the distinct advantage that as many items of data can be added as required and no tally needs to be kept of how many items are in the list. If the end of the data is indicated by ZZZZ, the following additional lines perform the checking.

```
 60 READ eng$ : IF eng$ = "ZZZZ" THEN END
 65 READ fr$
30000 DATA "ZZZZ"
```

6.3 iv. As everyone is motivated to some extent by reward, it is a good idea to display an indication of success at the end of a test program. With our test program we now allow the user, if he so desires, to see the result without trying and he may also try as many times as he likes. An indication of success could be the number of items found successfully on the first attempt compared with the total number of items. One way would be to keep a temporary counter to check on the number of attempts on the current item. If the number of times he moves onto the next item is counted, with the attempt count equal to 1, there is a tally of how many first time successes he has. The number of items also needs to be counted. One of the many possible versions of a program which does this is:

```
 10 PRINT"This program tests your knowledge"
 20 PRINT"of French. It prints an English"
 30 PRINT"word(s) on the screen and then waits for"
 40 PRINT"you to type the French. Follow each"
 50 PRINT"French equivalent by pressing the"
 60 PRINT"return key"
 70 READ eng$ : IF eng$ = "ZZZZ" THEN 180
 80 READ fr$
 90 tries = 0 : item = item + 1
100 PRINT"What is the French for ";eng$;
110 INPUT ans$
120 IF ans$ = "R" THEN PRINT"French for ";eng$;
    " is ";fr$ : GOTO 70
130 tries = tries + 1
140 IF ans$ <> fr$ THEN 100
150 PRINT "correct"
160 IF tries=1 THEN score=score+1
170 GOTO 70
180 PRINT"Your score is ";score;" out of";item
190 END
1000 DATA "A KEY","UNE CLEF","A KNIFE","UN COUTEAU"
1010 DATA "A DRAWING","UN DESSIN"
30000 DATA "ZZZZ"
```

Colouring the screen

7 Graphics: coloured text, points and areas

7.0 Introduction

An impressive outcome of modern computer technology is the moving display that can be produced. The BBC Microcomputer exploits this fully, and is widely acclaimed for its colour graphics. This chapter enters this fascinating area. It is concerned with such things as pictures, shapes and graphs, and shows you how to draw them for yourself. With a colour television you will even be able to control their colour.

7.1 The graphics modes

So far you have worked in a mode where you have seen only stationary lines of text with 40 characters on a line and 25 lines on the screen. The BBC Microcomputer has eight graphics modes. They differ according to the number of characters per line - which can be between 20 and 80 - and the number of lines per screen - which can be either 25 or 32. The number of modes available to you will depend on whether you have the simplest, unexpanded model of the BBC Microcomputer or the more expensive expanded model.

The more complex the mode, the larger the memory required. Amounts of memory are measured in a unit called 1K, which we shall not define. Sometimes the screen display alone needs as much as 20K. This memory, which holds data only while the computer is turned on, is called 'RAM', which stands for random access memory. The unexpanded model of the BBC Microcomputer contains only 16K of RAM and so you will need to add to it if you want sophisticated graphics. This is particularly so because, if memory is being used for the display, it is not available for program storage. So there may be times when there is a clash between the memory requirements of a long program and a complex graphics display.

With the unexpanded model of the BBC Microcomputer, you will have four modes available, modes 7 to 4. Modes 3 to 0 are available on the expanded model. The fundamental mode, in which the computer finds itself when turned on and with which you are already familiar, is mode 7.

We now detail some characteristics of the various modes. (We summarize these and other characteristics later in Table 7.1.)

Mode 7, the fundamental mode, normally displays text characters. There are 40 characters per screen line and 25 lines per screen. Mode 7 requires 1K of memory.

Mode 6 displays only text characters, 40 per screen line and 25 lines per screen, but it allows two colours. Mode 6 requires 8K of memory.

Mode 5 allows the display of 160 by 256 graphics spots which may be in any of four colours. In addition it allows 20 by 32 text characters. Mode 5 requires 10K of memory.

Mode 4 allows the display of 320 by 256 graphics spots in two colours. In addition it allows 40 by 32 text characters. Mode 4 also requires 10K of memory.

Mode 3 allows the display of 80 by 25 text characters in two colours. Mode 3 requires 16K of memory.

Mode 2 allows the display of 160 by 256 graphics spots which

may be in any of the 16 available colours. In addition it allows 20 by
32 text characters. Mode 2 requires 20K of memory.

Mode 1 allows the display of 320 by 256 graphics spots which
may be in any of four colours. In addition it allows 40 by 32 text
characters. Mode 1 requires 20K of memory.

Mode 0 allows the display of 640 by 256 graphics spots in two
colours. In addition it allows 80 by 32 text characters. Mode 0
requires 20K of memory.

To select a mode, use a MODE statement. For example, the
following line selects Mode 4:

        10 MODE 4

Whenever you execute such a statement to change the mode, the
screen clears.

The next section deals with how to select colours.

7.2 Colour in text

The computer is set to recognize colours by numbers, according to
mode. (With a black and white television, you should be able to
distinguish most of these colours as varying shades of grey.)

For modes 0, 3, 4 and 6 only two colours are available. These
are initially black and white although, as you will see later, they
can be changed. The colour numbers are as follows:

        0 = black
        1 = white

In modes 1 and 5 four colours are available which initially have
colour numbers as follows:

        0 = black
        1 = red
        2 = yellow
        3 = white

Eight normal colours and eight flashing colours are available in mode
2. Their initial colour numbers are:

        0 = black
        1 = red
        2 = green
        3 = yellow
        4 = blue
        5 = magenta
        6 = cyan
        7 = white
        8 = flashing black

```
 9 = flashing red
10 = flashing green
11 = flashing yellow
12 = flashing blue
13 = flashing magenta
14 = flashing cyan
15 = flashing white
```

Table 7.1 gives a summary of the facilities in the various modes.

mode	7	6	5	4	3	2	1	0
characters per line	40	40	20	40	80	20	40	80
lines per screen	25	25	32	32	25	32	32	32
spots horizontally	0	0	160	320	0	160	320	640
spots vertically	0	0	256	256	0	256	256	256
memory required (K)	1	8	10	10	16	20	20	20
colours available	Teletext features *	2	4	2	2	8+8	4	2

*(See section 11.11)

Table 7.1

The statement for setting text colour is COLOUR, followed by the colour number. For the foreground the colour is merely as given above. For the background, however, BBC BASIC requires that you add 128 to the colour number. The computer thus takes all numbers less than 16 as for the foreground and all numbers more than 127 as for the background. By way of illustration, the following three lines of program set 5 as the graphics mode, yellow as the foreground colour and red as the background colour of any text to follow:

```
10 MODE 5
20 COLOUR 2     : REM foreground = yellow
30 COLOUR 129   : REM background = red
```

Line 10 which sets the mode clears the screen to black. Also the statement CLS - meaning 'clear screen' - clears the screen, and makes the background colour whatever is set by the COLOUR statement. So the inclusion of line 40 CLS after line 30 would make the screen clear to red.

We will now give a program to write up a message and demonstrate the colours or shades of grey produced by the various colour numbers. It only writes in four colours to make it suitable for an unexpanded model of the BBC Microcomputer, but if you wish, you can easily modify it for all sixteen colours and mode 2 for an expanded model:

```
10 REM set up the graphics mode
20 MODE 5
30 PRINT"This is a demonstration program to"
40 PRINT"illustrate the colours/greys available"
50 REM use a loop to display all fore/background
      colours
60 FOR backgd = 0 TO 3
70    FOR foregd = 0 TO 3
80       IF backgd=foregd THEN 220
90       COLOUR foregd: COLOUR backgd+128
100      PRINT "Foreground = ";
110      ON foregd+1 GOTO 120,130,140,150
120      PRINT"black ";  : GOTO 160
130      PRINT"red ";    : GOTO 160
140      PRINT"yellow "; : GOTO 160
150      PRINT"white ";
160      PRINT"background = ";
170      ON backgd+1 GOTO 180,190,200,210
180      PRINT"black"   : GOTO 220
190      PRINT"red"     : GOTO 220
200      PRINT"yellow"  : GOTO 220
210      PRINT"white"
220    NEXT foregd
230 NEXT backgd
240 END
```

Line 20 sets the mode to 5 while the FOR . . NEXT loops together with the ON . . GOTO . . statements display the message about the colours in every combination of foreground and background colours. Line 80 removes the cases where no message can be seen because the background and foreground colours are the same.

7.3 Activities

----

i. Enter and run the program of the previous section which displays the colours available on the BBC Microcomputer.

With a black and white television, do you notice that the colours give an indistinct grey display? If so, try changing the contrast and brightness to make the picture more distinct.

ii. What effect would you expect from removing line 80? Try it and see.

7.4 Addressing pixels

In graphics modes 0, 1, 2, 3, 4 and 5, you may draw pictures, shapes and graphs. This is achieved by lighting up the screen a small area at a time in some colour or in white. The size of the area depends on the mode of the graphics. The smallest is in mode 0.

A computer display is made up of tiny points of light. BBC BASIC is written to allow a maximum of 1280 horizontally and 1024 vertically. Unfortunately the display on an ordinary television, with present models of the BBC Microcomputer, gives only half this number in the horizontal direction and a quarter this number vertically. The difference between the theoretically possible high resolution display and that which is available for by an internal scaling applied by the computer itself. You will always have to address the screen as if it had the theoretical resolution, i.e. as if it had 1280 addressable points in the horizontal direction and 1024 vertically.

The position of an addressable point is specified by how far across from the left it is, which is called its 'X coordinate'; and how far up it is, which is called its 'Y coordinate'. Thus the coordinate of a position at the bottom left-hand corner of the screen is 0,0. The X coordinate of a position half way across the bottom of the screen is 640. The coordinates of the centre of the screen are 640,512.

The smallest area which can be controlled is called a 'pixel'. Its size varies according to the graphics mode. To address a pixel, you only have to address one of the addressable points within it. Any one will do. It is rather as if you were writing to a firm which had taken over and spread into a number of neighbouring premises. It would not matter which one you addressed as the firm would be reached via any one of them. To carry the analogy further, it would be pointless to go to more than one. It is equally pointless to address more than one addressable point within a pixel. One is enough and any one will do.

We shall clarify by looking at each mode separately.

In mode 0 there are 640 by 256 pixels. As there are always 1280 by 1024 addressable points, a pixel consists of an area two addressable points wide and four addressable points high. Thus the pixel at the extreme left-hand corner of the screen contains the following addressable points:

0,0 1,0 0,1 1,1 0,2 1,2 0,3 1,3.

You can of course address the whole pixel via any one of these points. In any mode the pixel corresponds to the smallest point of light on the screen.

In modes 1 and 4 there are 320 by 256 pixels, each consisting of sixteen addressable points, four horizontally and four vertically. In modes 2 and 5 there are 160 by 256 pixels, each consisting of thirty-two addressable points, eight horizontally and four vertically.

The PLOT statement allows sophisticated graphics variations and enables individual pixels to be turned on or off. It comes in the form of PLOT followed by three numbers separated by commas. The first number controls the required action and the other two are coordinates. If X and Y are the coordinates of any point within the pixel, the following statements respectively turn the whole pixel on and off. (We shall explain the significance of the 69 and 71 later.)

```
        PLOT 69,X,Y
and
        PLOT 71,X,Y
```

7.5 Activities

_____

i. The following program illustrates how the size of text and the size of pixels vary according to mode. It demonstrates for just two modes: modes 4 and 5. The line it draws is one pixel wide. ('mode' is a variable):

```
  10 mode=5
  20 MODE mode
  30 FOR P=1 TO 13 : PRINT : NEXT
  40 PRINT "        ";"Mode ";mode
  50 FOR Y=0 TO 600
  60    PLOT 69,640,Y
  70 NEXT Y
  80 FOR I = 1 TO 2000 : NEXT I
  90 IF mode=4 THEN mode=5 ELSE mode=4
 100 GOTO 20
 110 END
```

Do you see a difference in the size of the text printed on the screen? Note also the relative width and length of the line. (This is discussed in section 7.13.)

ii. Change the step size in the FOR . . NEXT loop to try to draw the line as quickly as possible. (Section 7.13 deals with this point.)

_____

7.6 Colour and the GCOL statement

The GCOL statement controls how colour is written to the screen. It comes in the form of GCOL followed by two numbers. The first depends on the required action and the second specifies colour.

For graphics, as distinct from text, setting the colour of the foreground and background requires the GCOL 0,C statement where C is a colour number. As for text, the foreground is set using a number between 0 and 15 and the background a number between 128 and 128+15, according to the graphics mode. For example, in graphics mode 5 which allows four colours, the following line sets a yellow foreground:

        90 GCOL 0,2

The following sets the background to red:

        100 GCOL 0,128+1

The statement CLG clears the screen to the background colour.

The simple GCOL 0 statement merely sets colour or replaces one colour with another, and you will be able to achieve quite a lot with it. There are extensions to the GCOL statement which allow manipulations between colours. These are particularly useful for animation. They rely on logical operations of binary arithmetic, and we introduce them in the next section. If you are completely unfamiliar with binary logic, you may find the next section too obscure to follow. If so, just scan it and continue with the activities of section 7.8.

7.7 Binary arithmetic and extensions to GCOL

For animation in graphics, you need extensions to the GCOL statement. These are GCOL 1,C GCOL 2,C GCOL 3,C and GCOL 4,C where C is a colour number.

The statements rely on the logical operations of binary arithmetic. The logical operation is carried out between the colour number (0 - 15) which your program is about to plot and the colour number (0 - 15) already on the screen. The following are the binary equivalents, in 0's and 1's, of the normal numbers from 0 to 15:

        0 = 0000
        1 = 0001
        2 = 0010
        3 = 0011
        4 = 0100
        5 = 0101
        6 = 0110
        7 = 0111

```
 8 = 1000
 9 = 1001
10 = 1010
11 = 1011
12 = 1100
13 = 1101
14 = 1110
15 = 1111
```

GCOL 1,C relies on the 'logical OR' operation. The OR operation is such that:

```
0 OR 0 = 0
1 OR 0 = 1
1 OR 1 = 1
```

To 'logically OR' two binary numbers, place one below the other and apply the above method of combining the 0's and 1's vertically. For example 4 OR 5 = 5 as shown below:

```
       4 = 0100
       5 = 0101
  4 OR 5 = 0101
```

This means that if the screen colour number at the address considered is currently 4, then PLOT 1,5 will produce a colour number of 5 on the screen.

GCOL 2,C relies on the 'logical AND' operation. The logical AND operation is such that:

```
0 AND 0 = 0
1 AND 0 = 0
1 AND 1 = 1
```

To 'logically AND' two numbers, place one under the other and apply the above method of combining 0's and 1's in vertical columns as before. The following example shows how logically to combine 4 AND 5, which gives the result 4:

```
        4 = 0100
        5 = 0101
  4 AND 5 = 0100
```

This means that if the screen colour number at the address considered is currently 4, then PLOT 2,5 will produce a colour number of 4 on the screen.

GCOL 3,C relies on the 'logical EOR' operation. The logical EOR operation is such that:

```
4 = 0100
```

        5 = 0101
    4 EOR 5 = 0001

This means that if the screen colour number at the address considered is currently 4, then PLOT 3,5 will produce a colour number of 1 on the screen. GCOL 4,C relies on a logical operation which inverts by turning all 0's to 1's and all 1's to 0's, e.g. 5 (=0101) becomes 10 (=1010). This means that if the screen colour number at the address considered is currently 4, then PLOT 4,5 will produce a colour number of 10 on the screen. The colour number supplied by the PLOT statement is ignored.

    You can best understand the practical differences between the various GCOL statements by seeing the effects for yourself. You can do this in the following activities.

7.8 Activities

----

i. Enter and run the following program which draws a block of colour very slowly using the graphics PLOT 69,X,Y statement. It sets part of the screen to yellow and part to red, and then draws five bars across the screen using the 5 types of the GCOL statement.

```
 10 MODE 5
 20 GCOL 0,129 : REM background = red
 30 CLG        : REM clear screen to red
 40 GCOL 0,2   : REM foreground = yellow
 50 FOR X = 300 TO 500 STEP 8
 60    FOR Y = 100 TO 580 STEP 4
 70       PLOT 69,X,Y
 80    NEXT Y
 90 NEXT X
100 REM now draw bands using each GCOL
110 FOR band = 0 TO 4
120    GCOL band,2
130    up = up + 100 : REM sets the gap between bands
140    REM now draw band
150    FOR X = 300 TO 700 STEP 8
160       FOR Y = 0 TO 80 STEP 4
170          PLOT 69,X,Y+up
180       NEXT Y
190    NEXT X
200 NEXT band
210 FOR L=0 TO 14 : PRINT : NEXT L
220 PRINT"INVERT" ' ' ' "XOR" ' ' ' "AND"
230 PRINT ' ' " OR " ' ' ' ' "PLOT"
230 END
```

ii. Examine the colour of each band as it crosses the areas which
started as yellow and red. Note the corresponding number in the
GCOL statement and see if you can get a feel for the OR, AND,
EOR and invert operations. (See section 7.13 for an explanation of
each colour.)

_____

7.9 The PLOT statement

You have already used the PLOT statement as PLOT 69,X,Y to turn
on a pixel and learnt of PLOT 71,X,Y to turn it off. These are just
two of many versions of the PLOT statement. Its general form is
PLOT N,X,Y where N controls the action required and may have any
value from 0 to 87. This allows you to choose from plotting points,
drawing lines or filling in triangular areas. It also allows you to
specify the coordinates X,Y as relative to the origin or relative to
some other point.

To select a value for N, take a starting value of 0 and then add
numbers from Table 7.2, according to the action you require.

+ 0   for no plotting action

+ 1   for plotting in foreground colour

+ 2   for plotting using binary logic to invert
      the colour number for the existing colour

+ 3   for plotting in background colour

+ 0   for plotting coordinates relative to the the previous point

+ 4   for plotting coordinates relative to the screen origin

+ 0   for plotting a line

+ 16   for plotting a dotted line

+ 64   for plotting a point

+ 80   for filling in a triangular area between the current
      position and the last two (which the computer remembers)

Table 7.2

choice of n for PLOT n,X,Y
where n = 0 + one of the above numbers

For example PLOT 69 (where 64 + 4 + 1 = 69) plots a point (given by the +64) relative to the screen origin (given by the +4) in foreground colour (given by the +1).

The routines for lines and triangles are many times faster than using a FOR . . NEXT loop for simply plotting the equivalent pixels.

7.10 Activities

----

i. To familiarize yourself with the variations of the PLOT statement, write a program with the following three parts to it:

(a) incorporating a FOR . . NEXT or other structure to fill the screen with a uniform colour of yellow using just the PLOT 69,X,Y statement to set pixels.

(b) incorporating the line drawing versions of the PLOT statement to fill the screen with red.

(c) incorporating the triangle filling version of the PLOT statement to fill the screen with black. (See section 7.13 for a version of this program.)

ii. Run the program with a program line at the end to cause it to jump back to the beginning in a continuous loop. (Section 7.13 provides a suitable program.) In this way examine the difference in speed between the three methods of filling an area with colour. We expect you to be impressed at the speed of the triangle filling routine compared to the line routine, and seldom again to use the pixel plotting method of filling an area.

7.11 Some points to think about

a. Is the number of addressable points ever equal to the number of pixels available on the screen?
b. What change in X coordinate is required to move from one point to the next in each of the following modes: 5, 4, 2, 1 and 0?
c. What change in Y coordinate is required to move from one point to the next in each of the modes 5, 4. 2, 1 and 0?

7.12 Discussion on the points to think about

a. In the unexpanded model there are always more addressable points than pixels. It is just possible that, at a later date, a high resolution display might be made available.

b. The changes in X coordinate in modes 5, 4, 2, 1 and 0 are 8, 4, 8, 4 and 2 respectively.

c. The changes in Y coordinate is the same for every mode, i.e. 4.

7.13 Discussion of activities

7.5 i. The text alters in width because the number of characters per line is 20 in mode 5 and 40 in mode 4. The height of the characters remains constant as the number of lines of text remains at 32. The length of the line produced by the PLOT statement is constant as it is fixed by the addressable points in the FOR . . NEXT loop, and the addressable points are the same whatever the graphics mode. In mode 5 the width of the line is double that in mode 4 because there are half as many pixels in the horizontal direction.

7.5 ii. Drawing the line in the minimum time requires that the step size in the FOR . . NEXT loop is as large as possible, consistent with still addressing a point in each pixel. In both modes there are 4 addressable points per pixel, and so the step size in the FOR . . NEXT loop would best be 4.

7.8 ii. Consider the bands as numbered from 0 to 4, counting up the screen from the bottom.

Band 0. This uses GCOL 0 which sets the colour regardless of what was there before. The band is thus yellow, the colour set in line 120.

Band 1. This gives a logical OR of the current and previous colour numbers. On the left the number to plot is 2 and the screen is yellow (=2) and 2 OR 2 = 2 (= yellow). The left of the band is therefore yellow. The right of the screen is colour number 1 for red. 1 OR 2 = 3 (= white). The right of the band is therefore white.

Band 2. This gives a logical AND of the current and previous colour numbers. On the left the current number is 2 and the previous is 2 and 2 AND 2 = 2 (= yellow). The left of the band is therefore yellow. The right of the screen is colour number 1 for red. 1 AND 2 = 0 (= black). The right of the band is therefore black.

Band 3. This gives a logical EOR of the current and previous colour numbers. On the left the current number is 2 and the previous is 2 and 2 EOR 2 = 0 (= black). The left of the band is therefore black. The right of the screen is colour number 1 for red. 1 EOR 2 = 3 (= white). The right of the band is therefore white.

Band 4. This gives a logical invert of the previous colour number. On the left the previous colour number is 2, which inverted is 13. This is higher than the highest allowable colour number in this graphics mode. So the higher binary digits are ignored until the number so formed comes down to the allowable range of 0 to 3. This process produces 1 which is red. The left of the band is therefore red. The right of the screen is colour number 1 for red. 1 inverted gives 2 (= yellow) when the higher binary digits are ignored. The right of the band is therefore yellow.

7.10 i. The following is a program in three parts to fill the screen in colour using three different methods:

```
10 MODE 5
20 GCOL 0,2 : REM yellow foreground
30 REM fill screen using for . . next loop
40 FOR X=0 TO 1279 STEP 8
50   FOR Y=0 TO 1023 STEP 4
60     PLOT 69,X,Y
70   NEXT Y
80 NEXT X
90 REM now fill screen using line drawing
100 GCOL 0,1 : REM red foreground
110 FOR X=0 TO 1279 STEP 8
120    PLOT 4,X,0    : REM no action
130    PLOT 5,X,1023 : REM draw a line
140 NEXT X
150 REM fill screen using triangle filling
160 GCOL 0,0: REM black foreground
170 PLOT 4,0,0      : REM first point
180 PLOT 4,1279,0  : REM second point
190 PLOT 85,0,1023 : REM first triangle
200 PLOT 85,1279,1023 : REM second triangle
210 GOTO 20
```

Debugging

8 Graphics: lines and colour

8.0 The MOVE and DRAW statements

There are two statements which are particularly useful for drawing lines on the screen: MOVE and DRAW. DRAW draws a straight line from the last point addressed on the screen to a point whose coordinates have to be supplied with the statement. MOVE sets the coordinates for drawing from some other starting point, and is used before the DRAW statement. It can also set the starting point for other actions such as the triangle-filling form of the PLOT statement.

By way of example, the following is a simple program in graphics mode 5 to draw a line between the point 10,0 and the point 640,1023 which is half way across the top of the screen. The background is black and the foreground yellow.

```
10 MODE 5 : GCOL 0,2 : REM yellow foreground
20 MOVE 10,0
30 DRAW 640,1023
40 END
```

Line 20 produces no visible action but specifies the starting point for the DRAW.

The following is an additional program line to draw a second line from where the present line stops at the top of the screen down to the bottom right-hand corner, 1279,0:

```
35 DRAW 1279,0
```

Drawing a rectangle would require the following program where the four lines containing the DRAW statements produce the four sides:

```
10 MODE 5 : GCOL 0,2 : REM yellow foreground
20 MOVE 200,100
30 DRAW 400,100
40 DRAW 400,500
50 DRAW 200,500
60 DRAW 200,100
70 END
```

We will now show you a general purpose program to draw any shape that can be made from straight lines. Not only do the coordinates of all the points concerned have to be specified. There also needs to be some indication of which ones are to be joined. When joining, the DRAW statement is required; when not, the MOVE statement. We will indicate this by including, with each pair of coordinates, a third piece of data in the form of a 1 or a 2 to indicate whether or not the current point is to be joined to the previous. We shall give a name to the variable to hold this piece of data. We shall call it 'flag'.

Such a program can be written in many ways, of which the following is one. It draws the shape of a house.

```
10 REM A picture-drawing program.
20 REM coordinates of points are given in
30 REM DATA statements with a flag = 1 for
40 REM a move,  =2 for draw and =3 for END
```

```
 50 RESTORE 200
 60 MODE 4 : REM white on black background
 70 READ X,Y,flag
 80 ON flag GOTO 90,100,110
 90 MOVE X,Y : GOTO 70
100 DRAW X,Y : GOTO 70
110 END
200 DATA 360,320,1,880,320,2,680,320,1,680,400,2
210 DATA 560,400,2,560,320,2,520,380,1,400,380,2
220 DATA 400,430,2,520,430,2,520,380,2,720,380,1
230 DATA 840,380,2,840,430,2,720,430,2,720,380,2
240 DATA 880,440,1,880,320,2,900,440,1,340,440,2
250 DATA 360,440,1,360,320,2,340,440,1,440,500,2
260 DATA 800,500,2,800,540,2,720,540,2,720,500,2
270 DATA 800,500,1,900,440,2,0,0,3
```

8.1 Activities

i. Run the house-drawing program of the last section.

ii. Modify this program to include the possibility of drawing each line
in a different colour (or shade of grey for a black and white
television). You will need graphics mode 5 and the GCOL statement.
(We discuss this in section 8.11.)

iii. How many different colours can be displayed at once? (We also
discuss this in section 8.11.)

iv. Construct your own program for drawing some other shape, and
test it.

v. How would you draw a rectangular block which is uniformly filled
in with a specified colour? (We also discuss this in section 8.11.)

vi. Just to see what impressive effects can be obtained by drawing
lines in different colours, run the following program.

```
 10 MODE 5 : REM MODE 2 for expanded computer
 20 colour=0
 30 FOR outbox=0 TO 9
 40    colour=colour+1
 50    IF colour>16 THEN colour=0
 60    FOR inbox=0 TO 100 STEP 5
 70       box=outbox*100+inbox
 80       GCOL 0,colour
 90       MOVE box,box
100       DRAW 1280-box,box
110       DRAW 1280-box,1020-box
```

```
120      DRAW box,1020-box
130      DRAW box,box
140    NEXT inbox
150  NEXT outbox
160  GOTO 30
170  END
```

8.2 Mixed graphics and text

So far, you have used PRINT statements to write text characters to the screen. However, where text characters are to be mixed with graphics it is useful to be able to control where the writing is to be placed. This may be accomplished with the following extended form of the TAB function which instructs that the printing start at coordinates 23,10:

```
20 PRINT TAB(23,10);"HELLO"
```

There is a slight problem in that the X and Y coordinates in a TAB statement are not specified in the same way as for the graphics: Whereas the graphics origin (point 0,0) is at the bottom left-hand corner of the screen, the origin for TAB is at the top left-hand corner! To add to the confusion, the X coordinate of the TAB function specifies the character position measured across the screen, the first position being counted as 0, and the Y coordinate measures the line number counting from the top, the first line being taken as 0. As the number of lines and the characters per line vary in different graphics modes, the TAB function has to be specially tailored according the graphics mode in operation at the time. The following two programs illustrate such tailoring so as to print a message in the centre of the screen in both modes:

```
10 MODE 4
20 PRINT TAB(17,15);"HELLO"
30 END
```

```
10 MODE 5
20 PRINT TAB(7,15);"HELLO"
30 END
```

The differences between these two programs is due to the first being for graphics mode 4 which gives 40 characters per line and the second being for mode 5 which has only 20 characters per line.
  The next example illustrates the use of the TAB function in a program which draws axes for a graph and labels them. It is in graphics mode 4 which gives the smallest spot size for the unexpanded BBC Microcomputer. The axes are drawn bold by making

them wider than the minimum line width:

```
10 MODE 4
30 REM Draw x axis
40 FOR Y = 80 TO 84 STEP 4
50   MOVE 238,Y : DRAW 1200,Y
60 NEXT Y
70 REM
80 REM Draw y axis
90 FOR X = 234 TO 238 STEP 4
100   MOVE X,80 : DRAW X,1000
110 NEXT X
120 REM
130 REM Write X axis and Y axis
140 PRINT TAB(0,4);"X axis"
150 PRINT TAB(29,30);"Y axis"
160 END
```

8.3 The VDU statement for locating text

There is a facility for printing text characters at positions set by
any of the graphics statements. This allows extreme precision in
locating text. For instance it enables the points on a graph to be
represented by an accurately located + or x sign. It uses the VDU
statement which comes in the form VDU followed by some numbers.
The first sets what is called the 'VDU mode', and this dictates how
many further numbers are required.

VDU 5 instructs that all text be printed from the current
graphics point and requires no further numbers. VDU 4 cancels the
instruction and also requires no further numbers. For example, the
following program lines print a + sign from the coordinate position
X,Y:

```
10 VDU 5
20 MOVE X,Y : PRINT "+"
```

8.4 Activities

----

i. Run the program of the last section to draw axes for a graph.

ii. You may like to alter the labels of the axes. Try putting a
longer label on the x axis to see the effect of writing over a line of
graphics.

iii. Add to the program to make it draw a straight line from the end
of the x axis to the end of the y axis. (This is discussed in section
8.11.)

iv. Add to your program so as to give the message 'slope' in the middle of the line you have just drawn. Do this first using VDU 5 and then using TAB. (This is discussed in section 8.11.)

8.5 The VDU statement for changing colours

In the last chapter we listed the colour numbers for the various colours according to graphics mode. You can alter the relation between colour and number with the VDU 19 statement. This can produce very impressive effects. The form of the statement is as follows, where C1 is the colour number you wish to redefine and C2 is the number of the colour you wish it to represent:

        10 VDU 19,C1,C2;0;

BBC BASIC requires the ;0; to make the VDU statement compatible with programming much more sophisticated displays.

Irrespective of the graphics mode, C2 can be any of the sixteen colours that have so far been associated with only mode 2. They are listed in Section 7.2. This means that although you can still only work with four colours in mode 5, you can select them from the full range of sixteen. Suppose, for example, that you wished to work in mode 5 with green, red, yellow and blue instead of the standard black, red, yellow and white. You could accomplish this by the following two program lines:

        10 VDU 19,0,2;0;
        20 VDU 19,3,4;0;

In line 10, 0 is the colour number for the black that you wish to change and 2 is the number for green in the full range of sixteen colours. In line 20, 3 is the colour number for the white that you wish to change and 4 is the number for blue in the full list of sixteen colours.

This statement can provide particularly powerful effects, by making parts of pictures seem to appear and disappear instantly. For example, by defining colour numbers 0,1 and 2 as black and only 3 as white, any pictures constructed with colour numbers 0,1 and 2 are invisible. By simply changing colour number 3 to black, you can turn off the display. Redefining 2 as the colour number for white, turns on all corresponding areas which were originally black and thus invisible. By such a method, the four colours could provide four unique pictures provided they do not use the same pixels.

You can produce animation with such redefinition of colour numbers. We shall illustrate this with a program which seems to produce white bars moving vertically up the screen. The program starts by drawing fine horizontal bars in graphics mode 5 using each of the four colour numbers in turn. Then it defines just one of the colour numbers in turn as white while setting the previous to black. By continuously changing the colour number which represents white, we produce the effect of movement without having to redraw anything. This method can produce a speed of animation which is many times faster than redrawing each picture.

The program starts with a set of lines to give graphics mode 5 and to draw a series of horizontal bars across the screen in the successive colours:

```
10 MODE 5
20 REPEAT
30    colour=colour+1
40    IF colour=4 THEN colour=1
50    GCOL 0,colour
60    J=J+8
70    MOVE 500,J : DRAW 600,J
80    MOVE 500,J+4 : DRAW 600,J+4
90 UNTIL J >= 1280
```

The rest of the program cycles through the colour numbers 1 to 3, redefining each in turn as white and setting the previous one to black:

```
100 VDU 19,colour,0;0; : REM turns old colour to black
110 colour=colour+1
120 IF colour=4 THEN colour=1
130 VDU 19,colour,7;0; : REM turn new colour to white
140 FOR J=0 TO 500 : NEXT J : REM wait
150 GOTO 100
160 END
```

Line 140 provides a delay to slow down the apparent movement. Alternatively the program could be working away at altering one of the hidden pictures in the time between turning a colour on and turning it off again.

8.6 Activities

Enter the above program to draw moving bands. Run it and adjust the size of the FOR . . NEXT loop to suit the speed which you think gives the best animation.

8.7 The VDU statement for changing the graphics origin

Although for graphics, the normal origin - i.e. the position 0,0 - is
at the bottom left-hand corner of the screen, you can change the
effective origin to anywhere you like. This is accomplished by the
following statement:

VDU 29,X;Y;

It moves this effective origin, which we shall call x=0 and y=0, to
the position given by the screen coordinates X,Y.

We can illustrate the use of this statement by reconsidering our
axes-drawing program. Once these axes have appeared on the screen,
it is clearly much easier to use them to give the coordinates of the
MOVE and DRAW statements. The following program line moves the
effective origin to the point where the axes cross, i.e. X = 238 and
Y = 80:

160 VDU 29,238;80;

With this statement, the cordinates for the MOVE and DRAW
statements should no longer be given relative to the bottom
left-hand corner of the screen, but relative to the origin of the
axes.

We shall further illustrate the use of the VDU 29 statement by
developing a program to plot a series of points on a graph. We shall
arrange that, while the program draws the graph, it also highlights
each point with a little +.

First a few words about drawing the plus signs. A plus sign
consists of a short horizontal line superimposed on a short vertical
one. The following program line draws such a horizontal line of
length 2x at the point X,Y:

200 MOVE X-x,Y : DRAW X+x,Y

The vertical of the + requires a line of the following form where y
is half the height:

210 MOVE X,Y-y : DRAW X,Y+y

Now, back to drawing the graph. We shall assume that we have
been given the coordinates of the points of the graph as pairs of
values in DATA statements. The program has to read these from the
DATA statements. So the complete set of extra lines to be added to
the axes-drawing program are:

160 VDU 29,238;80;
170 RESTORE 1000 : READ Number_points
180 FOR J = 1 TO Number_points
190   READ X,Y

```
200   MOVE X-8,Y : DRAW X+8,Y
210   MOVE X,Y-8 : DRAW X,Y+8
220 NEXT J
230 END
```

The 8 in lines 200 and 210 controls the length of the bars of the +
signs.

8.8 Activities

----

i. Add the point-plotting routine to the axes-drawing program and run
it using the following DATA statements:

```
1000 DATA 6,160,148,310,236,490,394
1010 DATA 620,517,810,630,980,778
```

ii. These points are scattered about a straight line which passes
through the origin. The problem is to locate this line. Fortunately
there is a formula for the pair of coordinates X and Y which produce
this 'best straight line' when joined to the origin:

    X = the average of all the X coordinates of the points
    Y = the average of all the Y coordinates of the points

Write a few lines to add to the program to work out these special X
and Y values. Then add some more program to draw a line from the
origin to 2X,2Y. Run the complete program. Does this give a nice
appearance to your graph? (We discuss this further in section 8.11.)

8.9 Points to think about

a. Will a program which displays both graphics and text work in
   any graphics mode?
b. Does the VDU 29 statement redefine the origin for the next
   VDU 29 statement?

8.10 Discussion on the points to think about

a. Assuming you choose a graphics mode which allows both text
   and graphics, the graphics will always be reproduced correctly,
   but any TAB(X,Y) statements will have to be modified to suit
   the graphics mode.
b. No. The origin referred to in the VDU 29 statement is always
   the bottom left-hand corner of the screen.

8.11 Discussion of activities

8.1 ii. You can draw lines in different colours in graphics mode 5, but the only colours available are red, yellow and white. The program uses a code of 1 or 2 with each pair of coordinates to indicate whether a line should be drawn or not. If we suitably modify the program and add a code to represent the colour number for the colour of the line to the current point, it could draw in colour. We will call this number 'colour', change 70 and add an extra line 75 as follows:

```
70 READ X,Y,flag,colour
75 GCOL 0,colour
```

Now the background will be black by default and so a colour number of 0 will result in a black line to the current point. The only other modification is to change the data to include the optional colour number 0 to 3 as well as the present flag for moving or drawing.

8.1 iii. The number of colours available depends on the graphics mode. With mode 5 the colours are black, red, yellow and white. Mode 4 allows only the two colours black and white. Section 8.5 discusses ways of altering these colours.

8.1 v. You will remember that the fastest method of filling in an area with uniform colour is the triangle-filling form of the PLOT statement. For a rectangular block of colour, just four lines are required as follows. Assuming the coordinates of the corners are X1,Y1 and X2,Y2 etc:

```
100 MOVE X1,Y2
110 MOVE X2,Y2
120 PLOT 85,X3,Y3
130 PLOT 85,X4,Y4
```

Note that lines 110 and 120 must be specifying opposite ends of a diagonal. Otherwise the two triangles do not form a rectangle.

8.4 iii. The coordinates for the ends of the axes are 238,1000 and 1200,80. The statement in line 100 will end at the point 238,1000 and so a single DRAW statement to the other coordinate will draw a line from the end of one axis to the end of the other. It could be:

```
115 DRAW 1200,80
```

8.4 iv. To write 'slope' in the middle of the new line requires that you first find the coordinates of its midpoint. In graphics notation it is found by taking the average of the X and Y coordinates of the ends of the line. This gives the point 719,540. Writing to this point

is relatively easy using the facility of writing text via the graphics
coordinates. This requires the lines:

```
160 VDU 5
170 MOVE719,540
180 PRINT "slope"
190 END
```

For the same operation using TAB, you will have to change from X
and Y coordinates to character positions and lines down from the top
of the screen. There are 40 characters per line and an X axis going
to a maximum value of 1280 for this graphics mode. This gives 32
graphics points per character position and so the X graphics
coordinate of 719 corresponds to 22.5 character positions. In the Y
direction you will find that there are also 32 graphics addresses per
line of text, and so the line you require is 16.2 lines up from the
bottom of the screen. The character position 22,15 is where the
message 'slope' should be written. The following will print the
message at the centre of the new graphics line:

```
160 PRINT TAB(22,15);"slope"
170 END
```

8.8 ii. To work out the average X and Y values, you have to know
the sum of all the X and Y values and how many there are. The sum
is easily obtained using an extra line, somewhere in the FOR . .
NEXT loop, as for example:

```
215 TotalX = TotalX + X : TotalY = TotalY + Y
```

You need a line earlier in the program and before the FOR . .
NEXT loop, setting TotalX and TotalY to zero. The number of
values is given by the loop variable J less 1. The average X and Y
value is worked out by a line such as:

```
230 X = TotalX/(J-1) : Y = TotalY/(J-1)
```

The line from the origin to 2X,2Y could be produced by:

```
240 MOVE 0,0 : DRAW 2*X,2*Y
```

Computer games

9 Animation for games

9.0 Introduction

On the cinema and television screen, movement is simulated by
projecting a series of still pictures, one after the other, sufficiently

rapidly to trick the eye into thinking that it sees continuous movement. You saw in the last chapter how to achieve this effect by redefining the colour numbers. In this chapter you will find another way of producing it: by continuously writing new graphics to the screen while removing the old.

9.1 A moving line

We shall start with a program to draw a line which lengthens while you watch. The program needs to identify the next pixel to light up, to light it up, and then to keep repeating the operation.

The PLOT 69 statement is best for lighting the pixels. It needs to be continually supplied with x and y coordinates which keep changing to be ahead of themselves. The simplest way is to increment the coordinates in the line above each PLOT statement in the following way:

```
120 X = X + 8 : Y = Y + 8
200 PLOT 69,X,Y
```

Provided that 8 is an appropriate increment, each time this pair of lines is executed, the line lengthens by one pixel, one further up the screen and to the right.

When the line reaches the edge of the screen, line 120 supplies values such that the PLOT statement tries to light up a pixel which is off the screen. The head of the line then disappears. To stop this, you can rewrite line 120 in terms of increments, incX and incY. Then you can introduce some program lines to check for the size of X and Y and make sure that when they are about to become too large, the increments become negative. Lines 100 and 110 do this in the following modified program:

```
100 IF X>1271 THEN incX=-incX
110 IF Y>1015 THEN incY=-incY
120 X = X + incX : Y = Y + incY
130 PLOT 69,X,Y
```

This program draws a line which can be seen to extend up to the top right of the screen and back.

However with negative values for incX and incY there will be problems when X and Y eventually become negative. You can check for this and accordingly change the sign of incX or incY. The result is the following program which draws a line which lengthens continuously and bounces off the edges of the graphics area:

```
90 X=10 : Y=10 : incX=8 : incY=8
100 IF X>1271 OR X<8 THEN incX=-incX
110 IF Y>1015 OR Y<8 THEN incY=-incY
120 X = X + incX : Y = Y + incY
```

```
130 PLOT 69,X,Y
140 GOTO 100
```

Line 90 sets the starting position for the extending line.

9.2 Activities

----

i. Add a line to the beginning of the program at the end of the last section to define the graphics mode in which you wish to work. Depending on this mode, modify the size of the increment to make sure that a new pixel is addressed each time the values of X and Y are altered. Enter and run the program. Does the screen fill up with a line which bounces off the edges of the screen?

ii. Modify and run the program in another graphics mode. In which does the screen fill most quickly?

iii. Can you think of a method of rubbing out the line just a little way behind the point at which it is being written? (We discuss this in the next section.)

9.3 An animated snake

In this section we help you to produce a program to draw a snake moving round the screen. For its head, you can use the program that we have already developed. For its tail, you need extra program lines to rub out a short distance behind the head.

   PLOT 71 is most appropriate for rubbing out, as it plots in the background colour. The next step is to identify where to rub out, which is simple because you can use the same type of calculation as for the writing. You merely have to start the writing at a different point from the rubbing out.

   By way of illustration, the following program results in a snake-like line being written to the screen. Writing to the screen starts at a point 320 units along the x and y axes ahead of the rubbing out.

```
10 MODE 5
20 GCOL0,2 : REM plot in yellow
30 GCOL 0,129 : REM red background
40 CLG
50 REM
60 DX=330 : DY=330 : incX=8 : incY=8
70 RubX=10 : RubY=10 : incXX=8 : incYY=8
80 PLOT 69,DX,DY
```

```
 90 IF DX>1271 OR DX<8 THEN incX=-incX
100 IF DY>1015 OR DY<8 THEN incY=-incY
110 DX = DX + incX : DY = DY + incY
120 PLOT 71,RubX,RubY
130 REM
140 REM
150 IF RubX>1271 OR RubX<8 THEN incXX=-incXX
160 IF RubY>1015 OR RubY<8 THEN incYY=-incYY
170 RubX = RubX + incXX : RubY = RubY + incYY
180 GOTO 80
190 END
```

You will probably have spotted how the empty REM statements in
lines 50, 130 and 140 visually break the program up into meaningful
sections.

9.4 Activities

---

i. Enter and run the snake program. How can you modify it to halve
the snake's length? (Section 9.15 deals with this point.)

ii. Making the snake very long requires some careful thought. How
long can you make it and still be able to rub out its tail? (Section
9.15 also deals with this point.)

iii. The snake program makes the snake always travel up and across
the screen at the same angle. Experiment and see how you can alter
this.

9.5 A bouncing ball

The technique for bouncing a ball is similar to that for animating the
snake. The main difference is that only one pixel need be lit up at a
time, which makes the program easier to write. So far you have
written each new point before removing the old. Now you have to
blank out the old before writing the new, which means that only one
set of calculations need be in use at a time.

The ball-bouncing program is therefore very similar to the first
part of the snake program. The complete program is as follows with
the additional line, line 120, to rub out the previous point before
moving on to the next:

```
10 MODE 5
20 GCOL 0,2 : REM plot in yellow
30 GCOL 0,129 : REM red background
```

```
40 CLG
50 REM omit lines 20 and 30 for black and white TV
60 REM
70 REM
80 rubX=10 : rubY=10 : incXX=8 : incYY=8
90 X=330 : Y=330 : incX=8 : incY=8
100 IF X>1271 OR X<8 THEN incX=-incX
110 IF Y>1015 OR Y<8 THEN incY=-incY
120 PLOT 71,X,Y
130 X = X + incX : Y = Y + incY
140 PLOT 69,X,Y
150 GOTO 100
```

One point deserves attention. In continuously lighting up and removing pixels, there are periods of brightness and darkness. Animation is most realistic if the former is long compared with the latter. Thus the gap in the program between rubbing out and rewriting should be as short as possible and the gap between writing and rubbing out should be much longer. To achieve this, you must take care to have the time-consuming lines between those for the lighting up and rubbing out. Lack of attention to this sort of detail reduces the impact of the display.

9.6 Activities

----

i. Enter and run the bouncing ball program in mode 5. If your computer has a mode offering a higher resolution, accordingly modify the program and re-run it. Do you notice that the ball is less distinct in the higher resolution mode?

ii. Put in the following new lines which place most of the time consumed by the calculation between the rubbing out and the next lighting up:

```
95 PLOT 69,X,Y
150 GOTO 95
```

What differences do you expect to see in the display? Run the program and see if you notice any difference.

9.7 Bouncing and nibbling away

We now turn to a further animation which can be introduced into the ball-bouncing display. When an object is in the ball's way, the ball can be made to nibble a bit away as it bounces.

The procedure relies on the function POINT(X,Y) which evaluates the colour number of the point X,Y. (The function gives -1 for a position off the screen.) You can use the function to test the colour of the point just ahead of the ball. If this turns out to be the background colour, the ball must still be in flight. Only when the colour is that of the object, is the ball about to hit. Once you have detected the imminent impact, you can program accordingly. A change of direction will give the appearance of a bounce, and returning the point of impact to the background colour will give the appearance of the object being nibbled away.

Programs to bounce and nibble are very similar to those we have already introduced. The exception is that you must now add the test to see if the ball is about to hit a non-background colour. The following line makes this test:

110 IF POINT(X+incX,Y+incY) = backcolour THEN . . . .

If background colour is ahead of the ball, then it should keep going in the same direction. This is allowed for by a conditional jump to later in the program.

The next lines are then only executed if a non-background colour is ahead, i.e. when there should be a bounce.

With impact iminent the program must decide whether the motion in the x or the y direction or both must be reversed. Line 140 makes this test for the x direction and alters the sign of the increment as appropriate.

140 IF POINT(X+incX,Y) <> back THEN incX=-incX

Similarly a test must be made by the program to see if the motion in the y direction needs reversing. The following line 150 arranges to do this:

150 IF POINT(X,Y+incY) <> back THEN incY=-incY

The program then nibbles all around the area from which it bounced, using the triangle form of the PLOT statement with the plotting colour set to background, i.e. PLOT 87.

The program continues with the lines for normal motion when no bounce is imminent.

160 X=X+incX : Y=Y+incY
170 PLOT 69,X,Y

For a complete program you need some program lines to draw the object. Let it be some vertical bars and some writing. These can be drawn with the following lines:

10 MODE 5 : GCOL 0,129 : COLOUR 129 : CLG :
REM red background

```
20 GCOL 0,2 : REM plot in yellow
30 FOR X = 100 TO 1280 STEP 100
40    MOVE X,200  : MOVE X+20,200
50    PLOT 85,X,900 : PLOT 85,X+20,900
60 NEXT X
70 PRINT TAB(0,28);"PROGRAM NIBBLE AWAY"
```

(For a black and white television, it is clearer to use GCOL 0,3 in line 10, to plot in white.)

This triangle-filling method is the fastest for drawing the bars. Line 40 sets up the first two points for the triangle-drawing routine in line 50. The surrounding FOR . . NEXT loop makes the bars 100 graphics units apart.

The following is the complete program. It draws bars on the screen and a ball bouncing around nibbling them away at each bounce:

```
10 MODE 5 : GCOL 0,129 : COLOUR 129 : CLG :
   REM red background
20 GCOL 0,2 : REM plot in yellow
30 FOR X = 100 TO 1280 STEP 100
40    MOVE X,200  : MOVE X+20,200
50    PLOT 85,X,900 : PLOT 85,X+20,900
60 NEXT X
70 PRINT TAB(0,28);"PROGRAM NIBBLE AWAY"
80 X=30 : Y=600 : back=1 : GCOL 0,3
90 incX=8 : incY=8
100 REM check what is ahead
110 IF POINT(X+incX,Y+incY) =  back THEN 190
120 REM object ahead so determine
130 REM which inc needs reversing
140 IF POINT(X+incX,Y)<>back THEN incX=-incX
150 IF POINT(X,Y+incY)<>back THEN incY=-incY
160 REM now erase all around
170 MOVE X-8,Y-8 : MOVE X+8,Y-8
180 PLOT 87,X-8,Y+8 : PLOT 87,X+8,Y+8
190 REM erase old ball
200 PLOT 71,X,Y
210 REM
220 REM
230 REM alter X and Y for new position
240 X=X+incX : Y=Y+incY
250 REM plot new ball position
260 PLOT 69,X,Y
270 GOTO 100
```

9.8 Activities

Enter and run the complete program of the previous section to draw
bars on the screen and have a ball bouncing around nibbling them
away at each bounce. Does it run as you expect?

9.9 Beginning competitive games

For many games, particularly competitive ones, time is important.
For example, you may well want the computer to make some instant
response as soon as someone presses a key, without the delay of
their having to press the return key. To accommodate this, there is
a function which detects the mere pressing of a key. It comes in two
forms.
    The first is GET. It waits for a key to be pressed and then
provides the program with the value corresponding to the key. It is
used in the form X=GET for a number or X$=GET$ for a string.
If no key is pressed, it causes the program to wait for ever.
    The second form of the function waits for a specified time for a
key to be pressed. If a key is not pressed within this time, it gives
a zero value and causes the next statement in the program to be
executed. The function is written as X=INKEY(20) for a number or
X$=INKEY$(10) for a string, where the number in brackets indicates
the waiting time. This is measured in hundredths of a second. So
X=INKEY(100) waits for 1 second.
    Another function is TIME. This is useful for measuring time, for
example how long a program has been running. It is incremented in
hundredths of a second and is called a 'pseudo variable' because it
does not stay at the value to which it is originally set but is
continuously increased by the computer as time goes by. To time the
duration of a program, you may start with a line such as:

      10 TIME = 0

You might follow later in the program with a line such as:

      1500 PRINT TIME

This prints out the time to the nearest hundredth of a second since
line 10 was executed. For competitive games you may wish to ensure
that a player is allowed no more than a certain time. A simple test
of the value of TIME allows the program to end when the time is
up, perhaps with the score being printed.
    Another useful function for competitive games is RND which
provides a random number. In a program you might use it in the
form X=RND(10) where it will give X a random integer value

between 1 and 10 inclusive. If you want a random decimal value, use
X=RND(1) which will give a random number in the range from 0 to
0.99999999. There is always the query of exactly how random a
random number is - but we will not get involved in this debate!
However, if you are worried about randomness, the first line in your
program can set the random number generator in a random fashion
with the following line:

        10 X=RND(-TIME)

9.10 Activities

----

i. The following program can test a person's ability to find the
correct key on the keyboard in a given time. It illustrates the use of
INKEY, RND and TIME, and incidentally may also help to improve
your typing speed! In writing it, we have had to call upon a feature
of BASIC which we cannot explain until later in the book. (See
lines 180 and 190 where CHR$ generates a letter of the alphabet.)
Enter and run the program, noting that lines 30 to 110 end with a
single quote for a new line.

```
 10 MODE 5 : COLOUR 129 : CLS: REM set red background
 20 COLOUR 2 : REM yellow writing
 30 PRINT"This is a reaction'"
 40 PRINT"test. A letter will'"
 50 PRINT"appear at the'"
 60 PRINT"centre of the'"
 70 PRINT"screen. When it'"
 80 PRINT"does, press that'"
 90 PRINT"key. After 20 tries,'"
100 PRINT"your score will be'"
110 PRINT"displayed'"
120 INPUT"READY",A$
130 REM set to white letters
140 COLOUR 3 : TIME = 0 : count=0 : hesitation=0
150 REPEAT
160     time = TIME
170     Letter = 64+RND(26)
180     PRINT TAB(8,24);CHR$(Letter)
190     IF INKEY$(1)<>CHR$(Letter)THEN190
200     hesitation=hesitation+TIME-time
210     count=count+1
220 UNTIL count=20
230 PRINT"Your reaction time"
240 PRINT"is ";
250 PRINT hesitation/2000;
260 PRINT"secs a word"
270 INPUT"Another go",ans$
```

280 IF ans$="YES"THEN 10 ELSE END

ii. Record a copy of this program for the next activities.

9.11 User-defined keys

You can, if you wish, define the action of the ten red keys along the top of the keyboard so that pressing any one is equivalent to some more lengthy operation. This might be anything that can normally be entered from the keyboard, e.g. LIST, RUN, a statement, the function of another key, or even a group of program lines. Suppose you want merely to press key number 4, to run a program, instead of having to type and enter RUN. You could define the action for the key with the following line where the pair of double quotes surrounds the required action and ¦M represents pressing the return key:

*KEY4"RUN¦M"

Redefining keys is particularly useful for programming games. For example, you may like to redefine a key to be equivalent to typing and entering YES. You can redefine several keys at a time and even arrange for the meaning of each to be displayed at the bottom of the screen. Then much of the user's response could be by single key entry. You can also, if you wish, change the definition of a key within a program.

9.12 Activities

To familiarize yourself with user-defined keys, load the program which you saved from the last activities. Define the first two keys (0 and 1) as 'RUN' and 'LIST' as we described in the previous section. Try the keys to check that they have been redefined correctly.

9.13 Some points to think about

a. Which graphics mode is most suitable for the ball-bouncing program?

9.14 Discussion on the points to think about

a. There needs to be some compromise over which is the 'best' mode. In graphics mode 4, which in the unexpanded model has the highest resolution, the pixels are very small. Although this results in a smooth motion, the display is not very bright. In a graphics mode with poorer resolution, the brightness is increased, but the motion becomes more jerky. The speed is also increased, provided you adjust the increment size to match the resolution by ensuring that a new pixel is lit every time the program goes through one cycle. Essentially you will have to choose the graphics mode to suit your own preferences.

9.15 Discussion of activities

9.4 i. To make the line half as long merely requires that the head is set only half as far ahead at the start of the program as is the rubbing out position, i.e. the tail. Thus line 60 should be changed to:

        60 DX=170 : DY=170 : incX=8 : incY=8

9.4 ii. The snake can be made any length you specify. You must however ensure that the calculation for rubbing out the tail eventually follows the same route as the head-writing routine. You will need to think clearly if the snake is longer than the width or height of the screen.

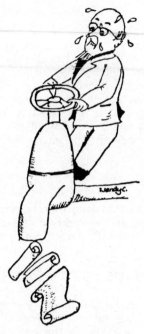

Running programs

10 Mathematical functions

10.0 Introduction

This chapter is concerned with lists and mathematical techniques. List-handling forms much of the basis for dealing with large amounts

of data and is fairly easy to understand. The mathematical sections
are more difficult and you may prefer to leave them until a second
reading.

10.1 Arrays

Everyone is familiar with lists: lists of candidates for the local
election, shopping lists, list of entries in a bank account etc. The
computer is ideal for manipulating names or numbers in lists. The
structures of such lists are called 'arrays'. We shall illustrate with a
list of the sort you might wish the computer to store if you were a
gardener. It contains vegetable seeds which are suitable for sowing
out of doors in February:

> Broad bean
> Broccoli
> Cabbage
> Celery
> Radish
> Shallot

An array allows a list to be referred to by a single name. We shall
call this one Veg.
      You tell the computer that you are going to use the list in the
form of an array, using a program line like the following where DIM
means 'dimension'. It informs the computer that you will be using the
name Veg to refer to the array and that there will be six items in
the list, numbered from 0 to 5. Each item in the list is referred to
by a number according to its position in the list. The $ is to show
that the array is to hold strings.

```
10 DIM Veg$(5)
```

Some BASICs allow the use of some small arrays without such lines
to declare them. This is not good programming practice. We advise
you to declare all arrays before using them.
      You could put the data into the array from DATA statements.
The following short program is suitable, where only J varies to
indicate which item is being dealt with:

```
10 DIM Veg$(5)
20 RESTORE 1000
30 FOR J = 0 TO 5
40    READ  Veg$(J)
50 NEXT J
60 END
1000 DATA "Broad bean","Broccoli","Cabbage"
1010 DATA "Celery","Radish","Shallot"
```

Once the program has read the data into the array, you can easily manipulate the list. For example, you could print it out in reverse order using the following three lines:

```
100 FOR J = 5 TO 0 STEP -1
110   PRINT Veg$(J)
120 NEXT J
```

Another manipulation that you can do with the list in this form is to swop round the order of two items. For example, the following lines of program swop Broccoli for Radish, i.e. item 1 for item 4.

```
300 R$ = Veg$(1)
310 Veg$(1) = Veg$(4)
320 Veg$(4) = R$
```

You could, if you wanted, write all this on a single line as follows:

```
300 R$=Veg$(1) : Veg$(1)=Veg$(4) : Veg$(4)=R$
```

You have now seen just two examples of how data within an array can be manipulated. There are many others. Items can be added or deleted under control of the program, and a list can be sorted into numerical, alphabetical or any other order. With an array, such manipulations are achieved through using just the name of the array. Without an array, the manipulation would be very difficult indeed, requiring a separate variable for each item in the list.

An array can contain numerical values. It is then no different from any other array except that its name must not end with $. The computer has to be told of the existence of the array with a DIM statement. The following indicates that there are going to be three arrays:

```
10 DIM Cost(10),Veg$(5),AGE(5)
```

Cost is an array holding up to 11 numbers, Veg is an array holding up to 6 strings and AGE is an array holding up to 6 numbers. You may write numbers or strings, as appropriate, in these arrays in any order. There is no need to fill them in any logical order because, as you will see in the next section, the computer can readily take on the task.

10.2 Sorting array items into an order

We shall now introduce how you may sort an array into alphabetical order. We shall use the Veg array as an example. As you saw in section 4.4, the following comparison will be true if A$ comes earlier in the alphabet than B$:

IF A$ < B$ THEN 100

You can make similar comparisons between two items in the array. If they are in alphabetical order and the value of J is less than that of K, the following comparison is always true:

400 IF Veg$(I) < Veg$(J) THEN . . .

If it is not, then swopping item I for item J would make it so. A sort called the 'selection sort' uses just this idea.

In the selection sort the computer is programmed systematically to compare the first item in the array with every other item in the array. Where it finds an item earlier in the alphabet than the first, it swops them. When it has been through the list once, the first item has become the first in the alphabet for the entire list. The process is then repeated for the second item in the list, the comparison only being made with items further on in the list. This done, the first two items are in alphabetical order. With sufficient repetitions of the process, the alphabetical sorting is complete. Although this may seem a very tedious way of operating, the computer is ideally suited to it.

The following program lines achieve the systematic comparison of a selection sort for the Veg array:

```
300 FOR J = 0 TO 4
310    FOR K=J+1 TO 5
320       IF Veg$(J) < Veg$(K) THEN 360
330       remember$=Veg$(J)
340       Veg$(J) = Veg$(K)
350       Veg$(K) = remember$
360    NEXT K
370 NEXT J
```

The first item on the list starts with J=0 and the comparison with the next item starts with FOR K=J+1 . . . The first item is then compared with all the others, which is why the FOR K = loop goes up to the length of the list 5. The outer FOR . . NEXT loop stops short of the end of the list as there is nothing with which to compare the last item. A similar routine can be written for sorting numerical arrays as may be seen in the activities of the next section.

There are many methods for sorting. The selection sort is easy to understand and simple to write, but rather slow for a long list. If you want to do much sorting, you should look at more advanced texts on the subject.

10.3 Activities

_____

i. The following program asks a person to type in a list of numbers.
It then sorts them with a selection sort and prints them as a list in
ascending order. Run the program and see that it operates as you
would expect. Then modify it to do the same operation with strings.

```
10 INPUT"How many numbers are you going to enter",num%
20 IF num% < 2 THEN 10
30 DIM N(num%)
40 INPUT"Your first number ",N(1)
50 FOR J = 2 TO num%
60    INPUT"Your next number ",N(J)
70 NEXT J
80 FOR J% = 1 TO num%-1
90    FOR K% = J%+1 TO num%
100      IF N(J%) < N(K%) THEN 120
110      R = N(J%): N(J%)=N(K%): N(K%)=R
120    NEXT K%
130 NEXT J%
140 FOR J% = 1 TO num%
150    PRINT N(J%)
160 NEXT J%
170 END
```

ii. Can you think of a method using two arrays, one numerical and
the other string, for sorting a connected double list such as the
following, first into alphabetical order and then into numerical
order?

```
3 Carter
1 Brown
5 Smith
2 Doyle
4 Hatter
```

Try writing such a program and get it to ask whether the sort should
be numerical or alphabetical. Get it to print out the list when the
sort is complete. (See section 10.11 for a version of such a
program.)

_____

10.4 Arrays of two dimensions

Table 10.1 refers to rainfall and temperature at Kew in London. You
could manipulate this data in the same way as the list of vegetable
seeds, but you would then require three arrays to hold the three

sets of data. Each one would be an example of what is called a 'one dimensional array' because it would be characterized by requiring only one variable to reference any item in the list.

Month	Rainfall (mm)	Temperature (degrees C)
1	61	5
2	38	5
3	35	7
4	50	10
5	50	13
6	49	16
7	64	18
8	63	17
9	52	15
10	55	12
11	62	7
12	59	5

Table 10.1

If you could store the three sets of data in a single array, you would gain a great deal of freedom in ease of manipulation. Fortunately you can. The array requires two numbers to specify each item: the first identifying its row and the second its column. For example, remembering that BASIC requires counting to begin at zero, the two numbers 9,1 refer to the number in the tenth row and the second column, i.e. 55. Since the array is characterized by two subscripts, it is called a 'two-dimensional array'.

Just as with one-dimensional arrays, the array has to be declared so that the computer sets aside sufficient storage space. The following line would be suitable:

    10 DIM Weather(11,2)

This declares the requirement of space for an array with 12 lines from 0 to 11, each with three columns from 0 to 2. To read the data in from a set of DATA statements would require lines of the form:

    20 RESTORE 1000
    30 FOR M = 0 TO 11
    40   FOR J = 0 TO 2
    50   READ Weather(M,J)
    60   NEXT J
    70 NEXT M

This corresponds to reading the table of weather information row by row. It would be just as possible to read the data column by column. You should decide which you prefer.

10.5 Activities

----

i. Store the weather information of the previous section in DATA
statements and write a program to read the numbers from them into
the array. Get the program to print out a list of the rainfalls,
starting with the lowest and going on to the highest, together with
the corresponding month and temperature. (We give a suitable
program in section 10.11. You may like to compare it with yours.
Which is shorter, neater or faster? How important do you feel these
differences are for you?)

Run the program, either yours or ours.

ii. Now write a program using graphics mode 5 to display the
weather data as a histogram with the month increasing horizontally
across the screen and the rainfall as the vertical columns. (See
section 10.11.)

iii. Once your program is working correctly, add a routine to draw a
line joining points representing the temperature for each month. Use
different colours for the rainfall and temperature. (See section
10.11.)

10.6 Mathematical functions

You are probably familiar with functions from pocket calculators.
Some examples are: square root, square, log, sine, tangent and cosine
(see glossary). BASIC can work out a value for functions in terms
of the value assigned to a variable. In other words, it can evaluate,
say, the square root of any appropriate number you provide it with.
For example, the following line causes 3 to be printed as the square
root of 9:

        30 PRINT SQR(9)

The function is said to have 'returned' the value of 3.
    In the rest of this section we shall be concerned with functions
involving angles. Examples include sine, cosine, and tangent:
SIN(R), COS(R) and TAN(R). For example, the following program
line returns the value of the sine of 1.23:

        10 X = SIN(1.23)

You may be surprised to see an angle written as 1.23, especially if
you have been brought up to think of angles in degrees. BASIC does
not recognize degrees, but requires angles to be in a unit called the

radian. (Incidentally a radian is the angle subtended at the centre of a circle by an arc of the same length as the radius.) For conversion purposes, a radian is equal to 57.295 degrees. A full circle of 360 degrees contains 2π radians, written as 2*PI (where PI is the ratio of the circumference of a circle to its diameter). The BBC computer takes the value of PI to eight decimal places as 3.14159265. Fortunately, it provides a means of converting between degrees and radians. This is another function, the RAD(D) function, where D is in degrees. The following is a line of program to give A the value in radians corresponding to 90 degrees:

```
20 A = RAD(90)
```

The following is a short program to print the values of the sines of all angles between 0 and 90 degrees in steps of 10 degrees:

```
10 FOR D = 0 TO 90 STEP 10
20    R = RAD(D)
30    PRINT SIN(R)
40 NEXT D
50 END
```

Or alternatively:

```
10 FOR D = 0 TO 90 STEP 10
20    PRINT SIN(RAD(D))
30 NEXT D
40 END
```

The variations of many of the angular mathematical functions are best demonstrated by plotting them on a graph. The following program draws a set of axes and then plots out the sine function for angles from 0 to 1440 degrees - which corresponds to four complete cycles:

```
10 REM a program to sketch out a sine wave
20 REM first draw X axis
30 MODE 4
40 FOR Y = 520 TO 528 STEP 4
50    MOVE 250,Y : DRAW 1200,Y
60 NEXT Y
70 REM
80 REM now draw Y axis
90 FOR X = 244 TO 252 STEP 4
100    MOVE X,100 : DRAW X,950
110 NEXT X
120 REM
130 REM now move origin to graph origin
140 VDU 29,250;525;
150 REM
160 REM now plot sine wave
```

```
170 FOR D = 0 TO 1440 STEP 4
180    PLOT 69,D,(400*SIN(RAD(D)))
190 NEXT D
200 END
```

The first part of this program is a modification of the axes-drawing program of Chapter 8. The step size in the FOR . . NEXT loops is such that each new value moves on to the next spot on the screen which can be lit up. A smaller increment in the loops would just have slowed the program down without giving any difference to the picture. Line 170 sets the range of the angle to plot. Line 180 does the actual plotting: PLOT 69 plots a point in foreground colour at the point whose coordinates are the next numbers supplied. The size of the printout is set by the multiplier 400 in front of the sine function.

There is a function, the ASN(S) function, for converting from the sine of an angle back to the angle. S is the sine of the angle and the result is the angle in radians. A conversion from radians to degrees is provided by DEG(R) which takes R in radians and gives a value in degrees. If, in a program, you have a value for, say, S as the sine of an angle X, the following lines return X in degrees:

```
10 R = ASN(S)
20 X = DEG(R)
```

or   `10 X = DEG(ASN(S))`

Further similar conversion functions for cosines and tangents are ACS(C) and ATN(T) where C and T are the cosine and tangent of an angle respectively. Both return a value which is in radians.

10.7 Activities

----

i. Enter and run the above program for plotting a sine wave. In particular, note how long it takes to complete.

ii. Mathematical functions always take quite a time to work out. Keeping the calculation time to a minimum requires that the quantity of calculations is itself kept to a minimum. The previous program did a conversion from degrees to radians for every point it plotted. This was time consuming and arose because the original FOR . . NEXT loop was written in terms of degrees. Rewrite line 180 to expect the angle in radians and replace line 170 by one which supplies the loop variable in radians. (You can use a mathematical expression when writing the limit and step size in a FOR . . NEXT loop. This means that for clarity the loop can still be defined in terms of degrees, even though the loop variable takes on a value in radians.) Does your new version of the program run any faster? (See section 10.11.)

iii. Try plotting out the shape for COS(R) and TAN(R). The
TAN(R) function has a value of infinity for certain angles. Does
this cause an error message?

10.8 More functions, logical operators

For the sake of completeness we now give some more mathematical
functions supplied by BBC BASIC (also see glossary):
    EXP(X) returns the exponential e raised to the power X.
    LOG(X) returns the logarithm to the base 10 of X.
    LN(X) returns the natural logarithm of X.
    ABS(X) returns the absolute value of X, i.e. it disregards sign.
For example:

$$ABS(64) = 64 \quad \text{and} \quad ABS(-64) = 64$$

SGN(X) returns a value which is 0, +1 or -1 depending on the
sign and value of X. For positive X it returns +1, for negative X it
returns -1 and for X=0 it returns 0. For example:

    SGN(123) = +1
    SGN(-123)= -1
    SGN(0)   = 0

INT(X) returns an integer value, i.e. one without any fractional
or decimal part. It produces the integer by dropping off the positive
decimal part. So it always rounds down and not to the nearest whole
number. For example:

    INT(10.9) = 10
    INT(-9.1) = -10

If you do require rounding to the nearest whole number, you can
use INT(X+.5).
    Another use of INT is to check whether or not a variable holds
a whole number. If a variable X holds an integer value then INT(X)
equals X; otherwise it does not. The following line would test for X
having an integer value because the statement after the THEN would
only be reached in this case:

    120 IF INT(X) = X THEN . . .

You have already come across the logical operators AND, NOT,
OR, XOR, MOD. The Boolean TRUE and FALSE are also available
but are beyond the scope of this book. (See texts on Boolean

algebra.)

10.9 Some points to think about

a. The program to plot out a sine wave produced a trace made up
    of separate dots. Can you think how an unbroken curve could
    have been produced?
b. How can a circle be drawn on the screen?

10.10 Discussion on the points to think about

a. The points could have been placed closer together by using a
    smaller step size in the FOR . . NEXT loop, but this would
    have made the program rather slow. Alternatively PLOT 5 could
    be used to plot a line for all but the first point. The curve
    would still appear quite smooth as the highly curved parts
    already have many plot positions quite close together.
b. A circle can be drawn in several ways. The following few lines
    indicate one method:

```
10 FOR rads=0 TO 2*PI STEP 0.05
20    PLOT 69,500+400*COS(rads),500+400*SIN(rads)
30 NEXT rads
```

10.11 Discussion of activities

10.3 ii. We propose a program which reads a list of numbers and
names into two arrays. It asks whether the printout should be in
numerical or alphabetical order. It sorts the arrays accordingly and
prints out the newly ordered list. The numerical sort, which comes
first, has been kept entirely separate from the alphabetical one. You
will probably be able to think of alternatives:

```
10 DIM num(4),name$(4)
20 RESTORE 1000
30 FOR J = 0 TO 4
40    READ num(J),name$(J)
50 NEXT J
60 PRINT"Enter N for number sort, "
70 INPUT"A for alphabetical sort"ans$
80 IF ans$ = "N" THEN 120
90 IF ans$ = "A" THEN 210 ELSE 60
100 REM
110 REM Numerical sort
120 FOR J = 0 TO 3
130    FOR K = J+1 TO 4
140       IF num(J) < num(K) THEN 170
```

```
150      R=num(J) : num(J)=num(K) : num(K)=R
160      R$=name$(J) : name$(J)=name$(K) :
         name$(K)=R$
170   NEXT K
180 NEXT J
190 GOTO 280
200 REM Alphabetical sort
210 FOR J = 0 TO 3
220    FOR K = J+1 TO 4
230       IF name$(J)<name$(K) THEN 260
240       R=num(J) : num(J)=num(K) : num(K)=R
250       R$=name$(J) : name$(J)=name$(K) :
          name$(K)=R$
260    NEXT K
270 NEXT J
280 FOR J = 0 TO 4
290    PRINT num(J),name$(J)
300 NEXT J
310 END
1000 DATA 3,Carter,1,Brown,5,Smith
1010 DATA 2,Doyle,4,Hatter
```

10.5 i. The following is a program to read in weather data stored in
DATA statements and sort into order of increasing rainfall. It then
prints the rainfall, together with the month in which it occurred and
the average temperature during that month. Note the use of a
variable C in a FOR . . NEXT loop in lines 130 to 170 to help with
the swopping of the data items from one part of the array to
another.

```
10 DIM Weather(11,2)
20 RESTORE 1000
30 FOR M = 0 TO 11
40    FOR J = 0 TO 2
50       READ Weather(M,J)
60    NEXT J
70 NEXT M
80 REM
90 REM
100 FOR J = 0 TO 10
110    FOR K = J+1 TO 11
120       IF Weather(J,1)<Weather(K,1) THEN 180
130       FOR C = 0 TO 2
140          R=Weather(J,C)
150          Weather(J,C)=Weather(K,C)
160          Weather(K,C)=R
170       NEXT C
180    NEXT K
190 NEXT J
```

```
200 REM
210 PRINT "      MONTH      RAINFALL   TEMPERATURE"
220 FOR J = 0 TO 11
230    FOR C = 0 TO 2
240       PRINT Weather(J,C);
250    NEXT C
260    PRINT
270 NEXT J
280 END
1000 DATA 1,61,5,2,38,5,3,35,7,4,50,10,5,50,13
1010 DATA 6,49,16,7,64,18,8,63,17,9,52,15
1020 DATA 10,55,12,11,62,7,12,59,5
```

10.5 ii. The following is a program to display the rainfall as a histogram of the rainfall each month for the year:

```
10 REM A program to draw a histogram showing
20 REM the rainfall at KEW.
30 MODE 5 : GCOL 0,129 : GCOL 0,2 : CLG
40 RESTORE 1000
50 DIM W(11,1)
60    FOR M = 0 TO 11
70       READ A,W(M,0),W(M,1)
80    NEXT M
90 FOR M = 0 TO 11
100    MOVE M*100,0 : MOVE M*100+80,0
110    PLOT 85,M*100,W(M,0)*8
120    PLOT 85,M*100+80,W(M,0)*8
130 NEXT M
140 END
```

Note the dummy read in line 70 to skip over the month number. We have done this assuming the same set of DATA statements as the previous activities which required a complete set of data. For the current program we assume that the data is written in the order of increasing month, and so there is no need to store this in the array.

You will also see that the bars of the histogram are drawn using the rapid triangle filling form of PLOT.

10.5 iii. The following routine gives a line joining the temperatures for each month:

```
140 GCOL 0,0 : REM Draw black for temperature
150 MOVE 40,W(0,1)*25
160 FOR M=1 TO 11
170    DRAW M*100+40,W(M,1)*25
180 NEXT M
```

190 END

10.7 ii. The replacement lines could be:

```
170 FOR D = 0 TO RAD(1440) STEP RAD(4)
180    PLOT 69,D*50,(400*SIN(D))
```

This allows the angle to appear as degrees in the listing. Yet the conversion to radians is done just the once when the program first executes line 170. This results in a slightly increased speed of execution. The remaining delay is due to the time taken to calculate the sine function, and cannot be avoided.

String handling

11 String handling

11.0 Introduction

You will remember that strings can be made up of any text, including punctuation and numbers, and can be up to 255 characters long. In programs they are represented by string variables which are distinguished from numerical variables by having dollar signs at the end of their names. This chapter is concerned with how to manipulate strings, i.e. extract parts, search for parts, etc. Its techniques form the basis of word processing.

11.1 INPUT LINE, LEFT$, RIGHT$, MID$ and LEN

Whereas a normal INPUT statement such as INPUT A$ can read in a string from the keyboard, it takes punctuation marks and certain other characters as delimiters rather than as integral parts of the string. The statement INPUT LINE A$ can overcome the problem. It allows all the entered characters, including punctuation marks, to be placed in the string A$. The string can be as long as you like - up to 255 characters - which is longer than the maximum for any program line. (This is in contrast to a screen line which can be 20, 40 or 80 characters long, according to mode.) Any keyboard entry which is longer than a screen line merely causes the typing to spill over from one screen line to the next, as you may have already seen. The typing is only accepted by the computer when you enter it by pressing the return key.

LEFT$, RIGHT$, and MID$ are three powerful functions for manipulating strings.

LEFT$ allows you to extract a portion of a string starting at the beginning and extending for as far as you specify. This is best illustrated in the following short program which extracts 4 characters from the string A$. Thus the printout is "hell" rather than the full string "hello".

```
10 A$ = "hello"
20 PRINT LEFT$(A$,4)
30 END
```

This function can help make a computer more 'user-friendly'. One of the main criticisms of computers is that they require responses to be typed in a precisely predetermined way. Thus normally only the programmer knows what the format should be, and only the programmer can run the program without trouble. For instance, if a required response happens to be YES, the program might not run with Yes, yes or the mistyping YAS. A user-friendly program would accept these alternatives. This can be arranged using a LEFT$ function because, as it can extract any number of characters, it can allow only the first letter of the response to be recognized. For example, the following section of program asks a question, and the next line checks to see if the first letter of the response is Y or y. If it is either, the program continues at line 130.

```
100 INPUT"Do you want to continue",ANS$
110 ANS$ = LEFT$(ANS$,1)
```

```
120 IF ANS$ = "Y" OR ANS$ = "y" THEN 130 ELSE END
130 . . .
```

You should always try to see how user-friendly you can make programs using this and other string functions. It is a matter of trying to anticipate all the replies that anyone might type as a response in a program, and then trying unambiguously to interpret them. Unfortunately, making a program user-friendly often takes a lot of program space and, in a book as short as this, we have been unable to make user-friendliness a priority in our programs.

The operation of RIGHT$ is similar to LEFT$ except that it extracts the right-most portion of a string. You again have to specify how many letters you wish to extract, this number being limited according to the length of the string. We illustrate with the following short program:

```
150 DEMO$ = "COPYRIGHT"
160 PRINT RIGHT$(DEMO$,5);" ";LEFT$(DEMO$,4)
```

Line 160 causes a printout of RIGHT, followed by a space, followed by COPY, i.e. RIGHT COPY.

MID$ is a more universal extractor of parts of strings than either LEFT$ or RIGHT$, and allows any portion to be extracted from a specified starting point. For example, the following program will print TEN:

```
110 EXAMPLE$ = "EXISTENCE"
120 PRINT MID$(EXAMPLE$,5,3)
```

LEN is a function which gives the length of the string. For example, the following line gives X the value equal to the number of characters in the string A$:

```
155 X = LEN(A$)
```

An example of its use could be:

```
50 IF LEN(ANS$) >3 THEN PRINT"Please
answer with YES or NO"
```

11.2 Activities

---

i. To gain some familiarity with the string functions before going to more complex manipulations, try to decide what the following programs do, and then run them to see if you were right.

```
10 A$ = "Hello"
20 FOR J = 1 TO LEN(A$)
```

```
       30   PRINT MID$(A$,J,1)
       40 NEXT J
       50 END
and

       10 A$ = "TOOL"
       20 REV$ = ""
       30 FOR J = LEN(A$) TO 1 STEP -1
       40    REV$ = REV$ + MID$(A$,J,1)
       50 NEXT J
       60 PRINT REV$
       70 END
and

       10 PRINT"Enter a sentence please"
       20 INPUT LINE sent$
       30 INPUT"Character to be taken out "out$
       40 place = 0
       50 place = place+1
       60 IF MID$(sent$,place,1) <> out$ THEN 100
       70 new$ = LEFT$(sent$,place-1)
       80 new$ = new$+RIGHT$(sent$,LEN(sent$)-place)
       90 sent$ = new$ : GOTO 60
       100 IF place < LEN(sent$) THEN 50
       110 PRINT"New sentence is:"
       120 PRINT sent$
       130 END
```

(See section 11.14 for a copy of the printout from these programs.)

11.3 A string search routine

As you will see later, BBC BASIC, unlike many BASICs, has a
statement which searches for a given string within a longer one.
Nevertheless, as it is so important to practise and become adept at
manipulating strings, we shall now explain how you can achieve the
same thing using only your existing expertise.

The first section of a program to search for one string within
another needs to read in both strings. It should check to see that
they are one or more characters long and that the given string is
really shorter than the long one. Then the program should set about
searching for the given string within the long one. After this it
should report on whether the search was successful and, if so, the
position of the given string.

The first part of the program should print up instructions on
the screen and accept two strings to work on. It could be as
follows:

```
10 PRINT "A program to test whether a short"
20 PRINT "string is present in a larger one."
30 PRINT "Enter a long string"
40 INPUT LINE Long$
50 IF LEN(Long$)=0 THEN 30
60 PRINT "And now the search string"
70 INPUT LINE Short$
80 IF LEN(Short$)=0 THEN 60
90 IF LEN(Short$) > = LEN(Long$) THEN PRINT"Search
   string too long" : GOTO 30
```

Lines 10 to 30 print the messages, while line 40 accepts the longer of the strings. Line 50 checks that the string is at least one character long, as does line 80 for the short string. Line 90 makes sure that the short string can fit within the length of the long one.

This first section of program is written so that it is impossible to feed in 'silly' data - an important point for all programs.

The next section of the program has the task of searching for the short string in the long one. We have written this section using MID$ to extract parts of the long string of the same length as the short one. A simple test can then decide whether the extracted portion is the same as the short string.

The extraction of part of the long string is done using MID$(Long$,J,LEN(Short$)) where LEN(Short$) is the length of the short string. The test and the string extraction can be performed on one line as follows:

```
120 IF Short$=MID$(Long$,J,LEN(Short$)) THEN ...
```

It only remains to make this test for all positions along the long string by means of a FOR . . NEXT loop as follows:

```
100 FOR J=1 TO LEN(Long$)-LEN(Short$)+1
110    IF Short$=MID$(Long$,J,LEN(Short$)) THEN 200
120 NEXT J
130 REM arrives here if not found
```

The last section of program must report on the success or otherwise of the search. If the program execution reaches line 140, then the search did not succeed. If the program arrives at line 200, the string has been found at a position J characters along the long string. The following is the complete program using these ideas:

```
10 PRINT "A program to test whether a short"
20 PRINT "string is present in a larger one."
30 PRINT "Enter the long string"
40 INPUT LINE Long$
50 IF LEN(Long$)=0 THEN 30
60 PRINT "And now the search string"
```

```
70 INPUT LINE Short$
80 IF LEN(Short$)=0 THEN 60
90 IF LEN(Short$))>= LEN(Long$) THEN PRINT"Search
   string too long" : GOTO 30
100 FOR J=1 TO LEN(Long$)-LEN(Short$)+1
110   IF Short$=MID$(Long$,J,LEN(Short$)) THEN 200
120 NEXT J
130 REM arrives here if not found
140 PRINT"String not found" :GOTO 10
150 REM
200 PRINT"The string has been found ";J;
210 PRINT" characters along the string"
220 PRINT Long$        :GOTO 10
230 END
```

11.4 Activities

----

i. Enter the first section of the string-search program in the form given below:

```
10 PRINT "A program to test whether a short"
20 PRINT "string is present in a larger one."
30 PRINT "Enter the long string"
40 INPUT LINE Long$
50 IF LEN(Long$)=0 THEN 30
60 PRINT "And now the search string"
70 INPUT LINE Short$
80 IF LEN(Short$)=0 THEN 60
90 IF LEN(Short$))>= LEN(Long$) THEN PRINT"Search
   string too long" : GOTO 30
100 PRINT"data OK"
110 GOTO 10
110 END
```

Run this program which will keep asking for a long and a short string.

ii. Try lots of 'silly' entries to see whether the program accepts them or whether it insists on your putting in correct data.

iii. Now add the rest of the string-search program and see if you can find any situations in which the program will not work?

Record this program before you turn off your computer as you will want it in the next activities.

11.5 The INSTR function

INSTR is a function for performing the search for one string within another. Its logic is much the same as that of the routine which we just developed in BASIC, but it is written in the much faster fundamental level of computer instruction.

Suppose you want to search for the string Short$ within the string Long$, starting the search at character X in the long string. The INSTR function is used in the following way, where P is the character position of the beginning of the short string:

> 90 P = INSTR(Long$,Short$,X)

When the search is to start at the beginning of the long string, a shorter form of the statement is suitable:

> 95 P = INSTR(Long$,Short$)

The INSTR returns the value 0 if it does not find the string.

11.6 Activities

You now have a method for comparing the speed at which BASIC works compared with the fundamental level of instruction inside the computer.

First, to see how quickly the INSTR function operates, enter the following program:

```
10 TIME = 0
20 Long$ = "This is a test sentence"
30 Short$ = "test"
40 FOR L = 1 TO 10
50    PRINT INSTR(Long$,Short$)
60 NEXT L
70 PRINT "Time to run = ";TIME;" centiseconds"
80 END
```

Run this program and see how long it takes to perform 10 searches for the string Short$ in Long$.

Now you can compare the previous timing with that for the BASIC program for the same task. In order to make a comparison with INSTR, you must remove the INPUT statements and all the printed messages apart from the one giving the position. You then need to surround the whole program with a FOR . . NEXT loop to force it to be repeated the same number of times, and you will see how slowly BASIC performs compared with functions written in the fundamental level of instruction.

Load the program you recorded from the previous activities and edit out all but the essential search lines. We have done this below. All but the essential lines have been replaced with REM statements and a FOR . . NEXT loop has been placed around lines 100 to 120. Run this close representation of INSTR and see how slowly it operates in comparison:

```
10 REM
20 REM
30 REM
40 Long$ = "This is a test sentence"
50 REM
60 REM
70 Short$ = "test"
80 TIME = 0
90 FOR L=1 TO 10
100 FOR J=1 TO LEN(Long$)-LEN(Short$)+1
110    IF Short$=MID$(Long$,J,LEN(Short$)) THEN PRINT J
       : GOTO 130
120 NEXT J
130 NEXT L
140 REM
150 REM
200 PRINT "Time to run = ";TIME;" centiseconds"
210 REM
230 END
```

We have inset the lines inside the FOR. . NEXT loop for appearance. Here we have found it expedient to jump out of the FOR . . NEXT loop each time the string is found. There is a limit to how many times this can be done without an error.

11.7 Conversion between strings and numbers

There are times when you need to make the number held by a numerical variable into a string, and similarly there are times when a string contains a number which you will require to lift out and use in its numerical form. The STR$ and VAL functions respectively provide these facilities.

STR$(V) takes the numerical variable V and returns the number it holds as a string. For example, it can convert the number 94.6 to the string "94.6". As an illustration, suppose you are writing a program to work out a bus timetable. You have the route number 20 held in the variable 'Route' and wish to make a string that reads "bus route 20". The following program lines achieve this and also print out the complete string:

```
125 Route = 20
130 Bus$ = "bus route " + STR$(Route)
140 PRINT Bus$
```

If you had as the starting point the string "bus route 20", you could extract the number 20 as a string using the RIGHT$ function as follows:

```
320 Num$ = RIGHT$(Bus$,2)
```

Having obtained "20" as a string, you cannot use it directly in numerical calculations. The VAL function converts the string "20" to the numerical value 20 ready for manipulation as a number. The following lines illustrate its use:

```
410 Bus_num = VAL(Num$)
```
Or
```
410 Bus_num = VAL("20")
```

The following line prints 40:

```
500 PRINT VAL("20")*2
```

11.8 Activities

Write a program to print out a message of the form 'bus route 20'. Make it able to substitute any number you wish in place of the 20 - to be supplied while the program runs, using an INPUT statement to request a number. (See section 11.14 for one version of such a program.) Run your version of the program.

11.9 The STRING$ function

STRING$ is yet another function of BBC BASIC but not many others. It provides a compact way of writing any string which is a repetition of groups of characters. For instance the following line gives a string of 20 'a's:

```
320 A$ = STRING$(20,"a")
```

It is equivalent to:

320 A$ = "aaaaaaaaaaaaaaaaaaaa"

The general form of the function is STRING$(N,A$) where N is the number of times the string A$ is to be joined to itself to produce the final one. A$ can be of any length but the final string must be less than 255 characters.

11.10 The ASCII representation

The computer holds all information - numbers, letters, symbols and punctuation marks - in the form of number codes. To give some compatibility between computers, a code has been drawn up to enable computer designers to use a standardized representation. This code is called the American Standard Code for Information Interchange, or ASCII. There are two string functions which allow conversion between a character and its ASCII code:
One is CHR$(V) which converts from the ASCII code number held in the numerical variable V to the character it represents which is a single character string. For example, the ASCII code for H is 72. This means that CHR$(72) is H so that PRINT CHR$(72) will print the single character H. The actual ASCII code extends between 0 and 127 whereas the BBC Microcomputer recognizes codes in the range 0 to 255.
The following short program will print out most of the characters available on the BBC Microcomputer by using a FOR . . NEXT loop to go through the ASCII codes and a PRINT statement to print out the corresponding characters:

```
10 FOR J = 32 TO 255
20    PRINT CHR$(J);
30    Count = Count + 1
40    IF Count = 16 THEN PRINT : Count = 0
50 NEXT J
60 END
```

We advise you not to use this function for printing values of J less than 32 because the visual display is very complex and is controlled by ASCII codes between 0 and 31. By trying to print these lower values, you will 'crash' the system!
ASC(A$) is the reverse of CHR$ in that it converts the first letter of the string A$ to the corresponding ASCII code. Thus if the string A$ = "HELP" then ASC(A$) = ASC("HELP") = 72 because the ASCII code for H is 72.
Programs to convert upper-case to lower-case rely on the ASCII codes. As an illustration, consider a program which allows the user to type in a sentence and print it with any specified word in upper-case and everything else in lower-case, regardless of how it is typed in. This can be done quite easily using the ASCII codes because the lower-case alphabet starts at code number 97 for 'a' and

goes through to 122 for 'z', while the upper-case alphabet goes from 65 to 90. Thus a program can be made to identify whether a letter is in upper or lower-case just by seeing the magnitude of its ASCII code. To change from upper-case to lower requires that 32 be added to the ASCII code for the letter.

We shall develop a suitable program. First we need some lines to ask for a short sentence, for which we will have to use the INPUT LINE statement as follows:

```
10 REM A program to take a sentence, print it
20 REM in lower-case regardless of how it is
30 REM entered and then emphasize any selected
40 REM word by printing it in upper-case
50 PRINT"Please type in a short sentence"
60 INPUT LINE Sent$
```

Next we need to convert any upper-case letters (ASCII code from 65 to 90 inclusive) to lower-case (ASCII code from 97 to 122 inclusive). This requires that we go through the length of the entire string Sent$ and, ignoring spaces and punctuation, make sure that everything else has an ASCII code greater than 90. The length of Sent$ is given by LEN(Sent$). So a FOR . . NEXT loop will allow us to step through examining each letter. The ASCII code for a space and for all punctuation marks is less than 65, and so all letters will have ASCII codes greater than 64. The following few lines will convert any upper-case letters (code 65 to 90 inclusive) to lower-case:

```
 70 Final$ = ""
 80 FOR J = 1 TO LEN(Sent$)
 90    L = ASC(MID$(Sent$,J,1))
100    IF L > 64 AND L < 91 THEN L = L + 32
110    Final$ = Final$ + CHR$(L)
120 NEXT J
```

Line 90 is not as formidable as it may look. It extracts the next letter from the sentence held in Sent$ and gives L the ASCII code for it. The next line, line 100, then checks to see if the letter is upper-case. If so, it changes it to lower-case. The string is reconstituted in line 110.

Now the program can ask for a word in the sentence to be emphasized. Having got the user to enter the word, the string search function INSTR can be used to find it. If it does not exist, an error message must be issued. The next few lines lead to this stage:

```
130 REM Ask for a word to be entered, convert
140 REM this to lower-case and then see if it
150 REM can be found.  Give error message if not.
160 PRINT"Enter a single word from the previous"
170 INPUT"sentence ",Word$
```

```
180 WORD$ = ""
190 FOR J = 1 TO LEN(Word$)
200    L = ASC(MID$(Word$,J,1))
210    IF L > 64 AND L < 91 THEN L = L + 32
220    WORD$ = WORD$ + CHR$(L)
230 NEXT J
240 Position = INSTR(Final$,WORD$)
250 IF Position = 0 THEN PRINT"No such word":GOTO 160
```

If the word is successfully found, then line 250 is passed, and
the rest of the program must now change the word to upper-case by
reducing the ASCII code for each letter by 32. For this the word
must be copied letter by letter. The end of the word can be found
by the presence of a non-alphabet character or the end of the
sentence. The program ends with the sentence being printed out in
full with the required word emphasized:

```
260 REM first extract the first part of sentence
270 SENT$ = LEFT$(Final$,Position-1)
280 REM now change next word to upper-case
290 FOR J = Position TO LEN(Sent$)
300    L = ASC(MID$(Final$,J,1))
310    IF L<97 OR L>122 THEN 340
320    SENT$ = SENT$ + CHR$(L-32)
330 NEXT J
340 REM add on rest of sentence
350 SENT$ = SENT$ + RIGHT$(Final$,LEN(Sent$)-J+1)
360 REM convert first letter back to upper-case
370 REM assume sentence begins with a letter
380 L$ = LEFT$(SENT$,1)
390 LT$ = CHR$(ASC(L$)-32)
400 Sent$ = LT$ + RIGHT$(SENT$,LEN(SENT$)-1)
410 PRINT"The sentence with emphasized word is"
420 PRINT Sent$
420 END
```

Line 270 copies the sentence up to the word to be emphasized.
Lines 290 to 330 convert the word to upper-case. Line 350 adds on
the rest of the sentence to make it complete once more. Lines 380
to 400 are needed to convert the first letter of the sentence back to
upper-case and line 420 prints out the final version.
    We hope this demonstrates how you, as a programmer, can tackle
any problem provided it can be stated explicitly and broken down
into small tasks.

11.11 Activities

----

i. We advised you earlier not to print out characters with ASCII codes less than 32. As, of course, you cannot damage your computer by doing so, try entering:

    PRINT CHR$(21)

Does anything strange happen? (This is similar to a crash because the display system is disabled.) Press the break or escape key to get back into the command mode.

ii. Enter the word-emphasizing program. Do so in stages, and test each stage for correct operation before proceeding to the next.

iii. Try writing a program to take in a sentence and then print out a list of all the words in it as a list in alphabetical order. (See section 11.14 for one version of such a program.)

iv. You may be interested in Teletext features because they allow coloured text and some coloured graphics in mode 7. They are turned on for any one screen line by a code and remain active for the rest of that line. The following program illustrates some of the Teletext features. Try entering and running it.

```
10 FOR I=32 TO 255
20    INPUT A$
30    PRINT I,CHR$(147);CHR$(I)
40    PRINT I,CHR$(I);"A short test message"
50 NEXT I
60 END
```

11.12 Some points to think about

a.   Distinguish between CHR$(48) and STR$(48). (Consider both how they are used and their ASCII codes.)
b.   Distinguish between VAL(B$) and ASC(B$). Consider both how they are used and their ASCII codes.

11.13 Discussion on the points to think about

a.   CHR$(48) gives the character corresponding to the ASCII code of 48 (which actually corresponds to the number 0). STR$(48) has the value "48", i.e. it gives a string.
b.   VAL converts a number held in string form such as "236" to a numerical value of 236 which can then be used in mathematical expressions. ASC(B$) gives the ASCII code for the first letter of the string held for B$.

11.14 Discussion of activities

11.2 i. The first program gives:

H
e
l
l
o

The second program gives:

LOOT

The third program gives:

Enter a sentence please
THIS IS A TRIAL SENTENCE
Character to be taken out
I
New sentence is
THS S A TRAL SENTENCE

11.8 i. The following is a program to form a string 'bus route 20', with the number supplied using a numerical value taken from an INPUT statement:

```
10 Bus$ = "bus route "
20 INPUT "What bus route is this",NUM
30 String$ = Bus$+STR$(NUM)
40 PRINT String$
50 END
```

11.11 iii. The following is a program which will take in a sentence and then list all its words in alphabetical order:

```
10 PRINT "Please enter a sentence"
20 PRINT "for analysis"
30 INPUT LINE Sent$
40 REM For convenience convert to lower-case
50 SENT$ = ""
60 FOR J = 1 TO LEN(Sent$)
70   L = ASC(MID$(Sent$,J,1))
80   IF L < 91 AND L > 64 THEN L=L+32
90   SENT$ = SENT$ + CHR$(L)
100 NEXT J
110 REM Now declare array for words
120 DIM Word$(30)
130 REM Find each word and place into array
```

```
140 Count = 0
150 FOR J = 1 TO LEN(SENT$)
160    L = ASC(MID$(SENT$,J,1))
170    IF L<65 THEN Count = Count + 1 : GOTO 190
180    Word$(Count) = Word$(Count) + CHR$(L)
190 NEXT J
200 REM Now sort alphabetically the array of words
210 FOR J = 0 TO Count-1
220    FOR K = J+1 TO Count
230      IF Word$(J)<Word$(K) THEN 250
240      R$=Word$(J) : Word$(J)=Word$(K) : Word$(K)=R$
250    NEXT K
260 NEXT J
270 REM Now print out list but avoid repetitions
280 R$=""
290 FOR J = 0 TO Count
300    IF Word$(J) <> R$ THEN PRINT Word$(J)
310    R$ = Word$(J)
320 NEXT J
330 END
```

In this program we have converted to lower-case; otherwise any word of the sentence in upper-case would be seen as different from the same word repeated later in lower-case. The conversion to lower-case in lines 50 to 100 is a copy of the lines used earlier in the chapter. Lines 140 to 190 extract the words by adding alphabetic characters one at a time to Word$. When a non-alphabetic character is detected, the variable Count is incremented ready to store the next word. The two loops in lines 60 to 100 and lines 150 to 190 could be merged together. We have kept them separate for clarity. The alphabetical sort of the words in lines 210 to 260 follows the selection sort described in Chapter 10. The display produced by lines 280 to 320 relies on more than one word being available and will only print one version of each word by using R$ to remember what was printed last.

Subroutines

12 User-defined functions and procedures

12.0 Introduction

As you know, it is easier to write and debug programs if they have a neat and clear structure, i.e. if they are broken down into recognizable and independent sections. Such sections may be of

139

various types. Three principle ones are called 'functions', 'procedures' and 'subroutines'. This chapter shows you how to develop or 'define' them for yourself.

12.1 User-defined procedures

A 'procedure' allows you to provide a statement of your own design. You give it a name of your choice, and it is then an independent section of program which you may bring into operation at any time through its name. We will illustrate with some examples. Consider the following simple program to print out N crosses on a line:

```
10 FOR J = 1 to N
20    PRINT "X";
30 NEXT J
```

If you wished to use these lines many times in a program, it would help to isolate them into a procedure as in lines 20 to 60 below. The procedure must have a name starting with PROC and must be introduced with DEF. The last line must be ENDPROC.

```
20 DEF PROCcrosses(N)
30    FOR J = 1 TO N
40       PRINT "X";
50    NEXT J
60 ENDPROC
```

This procedure informs the computer that there are statements in the main program, stating the name of the procedure and a number for N, e.g. PROCcrosses(8). Only on finding such a statement, should it go to the beginning of the procedure and execute it from from line 20 with N equal to 8. The procedure PROCcrosses would then print out 8 crosses.

There are two ways of calling up the procedure. Taking PROCcrosses as an example, either:

```
210 PROCcrosses(8)
```

or:

```
200 Num = 21
210 PROCcrosses(Num)
```

If the definition of a procedure is on a single program line, you may place it anywhere in a program. If it occupies more than one line, you should place it so that the program can never run into it unless it is called. We recommend placing procedures near the beginning of programs, so that you can see how they are defined before reading the rest. This requires a simple jump, before a definition of the procedure, to go round it. For example:

```
10 GOTO 70
20 DEF PROCcrosses(N)
30 FOR J = 1 TO N
40     PRINT "X";
50 NEXT J
60 ENDPROC
70 . . . .
```

12.2 Local variables

In the example for printing the crosses, we used the variable J in the FOR . . NEXT loop. It is always possible that this variable could exist elsewhere in the program. Then, having it in the procedure might catastrophically alter its value for elsewhere. To get round this problem, you may declare variables as 'local' to a procedure. This means that values of the variables on entry to the procedure are restored on exit from the procedure. When working with procedures, we recommend that you declare all variables as local, with a line like the following:

```
25 LOCAL J
```

Set within the procedure PROCcrosses, the line would ensure that the procedure would not alter the value of J elsewhere in the program. Thus if you wanted to print 5 lines of crosses as follows:

```
X
XX
XXX
XXXX
XXXXX
```

You would only need the following program lines:

```
200 FOR J = 1 TO 5
210     PROCcrosses(J)
220     PRINT
230 NEXT
```

12.3 Programming with procedures

Writing procedures is just like writing any other programs. We shall illustrate with one called PROCinput to clear the screen, write a message contained in M$ and then wait for an answer which must be either yes or no.

In the normal way, you could do this with the following program lines:

```
1010 CLS
1020 PRINT M$
1030 INPUT ANS$
1040 IF ANS$="YES" OR ANS$="NO" THEN 1080
1050 PRINT "Please reply with either YES or NO"
1060 FOR I=1 TO 2000 : NEXT I
1070 GOTO 1010
1080 REM end of this routine
```

You can convert these lines into a procedure by merely surrounding them with the following:

```
1000 DEF PROCinput(M$)
1090 ENDPROC
```

The procedure is executed using lines like the following:

```
30 M$="Do you wish to continue?"
40 PROCinput(M$)
```

Alternatively the procedure could be called by the following line:

```
30 PROCinput("Do you wish to continue?")
```

So far we have illustrated only one value being passed to the procedure - and this in the procedure's name. In practice, as many variables as necessary can be passed, both numerical and string. This is illustrated in all but the first of the following examples on procedures.

1. This example is a procedure to produce a pause of duration T centiseconds. We call it PROCdelay(T) and define it with the following lines:

```
2000 DEF PROCdelay(T)
2010     LOCAL time
2020     time = TIME
2030     IF TIME - time < T THEN 2030
2040 ENDPROC
```

2. This example is a procedure to draw a line of graphics. We call it PROCline(Sx,Sy,Fx,Fy) where Sx and Sy are the starting coordinates for the line, and Fx and Fy are the end coordinates:

```
5000 DEF PROCline(Sx,Sy,Fx,Fy)
5010     MOVE Sx,Sy
5020     DRAW Fx,Fy
5030 ENDPROC
```

3. This example is a procedure to draw a box with given coordinates. We call it PROCbox(X,Y,Lx,Ly), where X,Y are the

coordinates of the centre of the box while Lx and Ly are the lengths of the sides. It can conveniently call on the previous procedure:

```
6000 DEF PROCbox(x,y,Lx,Ly)
6010     LOCAL X,Y
6020     X = x - Lx/2 : Y = y - Ly/2
6030     PROCline(X,Y,X+Lx,Y)
6040     PROCline(X+Lx,Y,X+Lx,Y+Ly)
6050     PROCline(X+Lx,Y+Ly,X,Y+Ly)
6060     PROCline(X,Y+Ly,X,Y)
6050 ENDPROC
```

4. As a final example, a simple star can be drawn using the PROCline procedure. It can draw lines radiating out from a single point, each line of a fixed length and equally inclined to its neighbours. This is not as daunting as it may seem. A fixed line length and an angle can be turned into x and y coordinates using sines and cosines, and a simple FOR . . NEXT loop may then call on the procedure an appropriate number of times. The following program draws a star of 10 lines; R is the length of the lines in the star:

```
4000 DEF PROCstar(R,x,y)
4010 REM       x,y are the coordinates of the centre
4020     LOCAL Angle,X,Y
4030     FOR Angle = 0 TO 2*PI STEP PI/5
4040         X=R*COS(Angle): Y=R*SIN(Angle)
4050         PROCline(x,y,X+x,Y+y)
4060     NEXT Angle
4070 ENDPROC
```

12.4 Activities

----

i. Enter PROCcrosses and run it using the following lines:

```
10 GOTO 200
200 INPUT"How many crosses",X
210 PROCcross(X)
220 PRINT
230 GOTO 200
```

ii. Add the procedure PROCinput, of section 12.3, and then see if you can get the program to allow you to enter anything other than yes or no in your response:

```
230 M$ = "Do you wish to continue?"
240 PROCinput
250 IF ANS$ = "YES" THEN 200
```

```
260 END
```

iii. A number of the programs of earlier chapters could be converted to procedures. Modify the axes-drawing program of chapter 8 to allow the axes to be drawn using the statement PROCaxes. (See section 12.12 for one possible program.)

12.5 User-defined functions

You will remember that a function returns a numerical or string value as the result of some manipulation or calculation. For example, the function SIN(3.11) returns the sine of 3.11 radians.

If there is some function that you wish the computer had, and you can think of some program lines for the task, you can put them into your program as your own special function. For example, FNmean(A,B,C) could return the mean of the numbers A,B,C as defined by the following lines, where the FN in front of the name informs BASIC that what follows is not just a variable name:

```
1000 DEF FNmean(A,B,C) = (A+B+C)/3
```

With function definitions of more than one line, the end should be signalled by an equals sign on the last line, followed by the value the function must take. As an illustration, the previous definition could be written, rather wastefully, on three lines as follows:

```
1000 DEF FNmean(A,B,C)
1010 SUM = A+B+C
1020 = SUM/3
```

Many computers allow only single-line functions, which can be limiting. There is no such restriction with the BBC Microcomputer. You should always insert a jump before a multi-line definition of a function to divert the normal program execution. With reference to FNmean:

```
900 GOTO 1030
1000 DEF FNmean(A,B,C)
1010 SUM = A+B+C
1020 = SUM/3
1030 . . .
```

Functions can appear in PRINT statements, mathematical expressions, comparisons and most places where a normal variable name can appear. For instance the following are normal ways of using functions:

and
```
100 PRINT FNmean(a,b,c)
```
and
```
150 X = 100*N*FNmean(a,b,c)
```
and
```
A = SIN(FNmean(A,B,C))
```

The variable names in the definition of a function do not have to be those used to call it. What is important is that, when the function is called, it should have the same number and type of values or variable names enclosed in brackets as appear in the definition. The function definition takes and uses the values passed to it in an order that you, as programmer, define. You must make sure that when you call the function, you supply the values it needs in the same order as the function definition requires them.

Lines which define a function are clearly somewhat different from those which define a procedure. For a function, which has to conclude with a value, the last line must show an equals sign followed by an expression which can be evaluated. Also, whereas a program calls on a procedure by means of a statement which can appear alone on a program line, a function must appear within a normal program statement.

12.6 Recursion

Odd as it may sound, it is possible for a function to call itself. The process, which is called 'recursion', provides a very powerful means of solving certain problems.

Every time a function or a procedure is called, the computer has to remember the address of the line which called it. As this takes up memory, there is a built-in limit to how may times a function is allowed to call itself recursively. On the BBC Microcomputer, this is 33 times.

A classic problem which is simply solved by recursion is calculating factorial N, which we did in section 5.5 with a conditional loop. Factorial N or N! is written as:

$$N! = N*(N-1)*(N-2)* . . . 3*2*1.$$

The following program provides the function FNfactorial(N):

```
2000 DEF FNfactorial(N)
2010 IF N = 1 THEN = 1 ELSE = N*FNfactorial(N-1)
```

After the THEN and the ELSE, there is an equals sign. This means that the value assigned to FNfactorial is the value after the equals sign. The function keeps calling itself until the value handed on is 1, at which time the self-calling stops and 1 is assigned. The process then has to unwind, whereupon the whole series is multiplied starting with the 1, then 1*2, then 1*2*3 etc ending when N is reached, with the value of N!. If you are not careful, the recursive process may go on longer than the permitted 33 times and there will be an error message.

A line should be inserted to catch non-integer values and values less than one. The following is suitable:

```
2005 IF INT(N) <> N OR N < 1
     THEN PRINT "error" : = 0
```

12.7 Activities

----

i. Try writing a function to give the largest of a set of numbers. It could be called by a statement such as FNmax(a,b,c,d). (For further hints and a discussion, see section 12.12.)

ii. Enter the factorial function definition, together with the lines:

```
100 INPUT"Type in an integer between 1 and 33 "N%
120 PRINT"The factorial of ";N%;" is ";FNfactorial(N%)
130 GOTO 100
```

This program does not check for valid numbers. So try running it to see if it works. See the error message for supplying a number which is too large.

iii. Is the error for a number that is just too large due to (a) too large a final number or (b) too many recursions of the function? (This is discussed in section 12.12.)

iv. Write a function to return a Centigrade temperature from a Fahrenheit one. Call it with the statement FNcentigrade(F) where F is the Fahrenheit temperature. (See section 12.12 for an example.)

12.8 Subroutines

'Subroutines' are rather inferior alternatives to procedures. Since most computers do not allow procedures, you will need subroutines if you want to write a program to work on another computer - although if you want to transfer a program written for another computer to the BBC Microcomputer, we suggest that you replace all subroutines with procedures.

A subroutine is a group of program lines which is separated from the rest of the program. It has no name, but is called upon with a GOSUB statement. There is no clue to what it does apart from what you, as programmer, supply in REM statements. The same routine supplied as a procedure could be much more meaningful in terms of its name. There is another disadvantage. Variables may not be declared as local for subroutines. So you must be very careful to make sure that all variables have names which are unique. Many a program crashes because of lack of attention to this point.

We shall now ask you to examine a short program, containing a subroutine for printing out positive numbers with a space in front of each, and negative numbers with a minus sign instead of the space. There is, of course, no need to use a subroutine here. However, if the operation is required at a number of places in the program, the subroutine saves space. It is called by the statement GOSUB 1000 in line 50.

```
  10 DIM NUM(3)
  20 INPUT"Enter four numbers "NUM(0),NUM(1),NUM(2),
     NUM(3)
  30 FOR I = 0 TO 3
  40   N = NUM(I)
  50     GOSUB 1000
  60 NEXT I
  70 END
1000 REM subroutine to print +ve numbers with space
1010 IF N > 0 THEN PRINT;" ";N ELSE PRINT;N
1020 RETURN
```

The end of a subroutine needs to be marked with RETURN. This causes the program execution to return to the statement following the GOSUB, in this case to line 60.

It is important to make sure that a program cannot enter a subroutine except via GOSUB. For instance the omission of line 70 END in the previous example would cause the program to start executing the subroutine after the main program loop had completed. On encountering the RETURN, an error message would be issued as no GOSUB would have preceded the entry, and so it would have no address to return to.

Only 26 calls to a subroutine may be active at any one time. This is in contrast with the case for procedures where the number of calls is limited only by the memory available.

12.9 Activities

_____

i. Write the first two procedures of the chapter as subroutines. Design a simple program to test each of them. Run the programs to make sure that they work with the subroutines.

ii. See if you can write the factorial N problem using a repetitive call to a subroutine. (We discuss this in section 12.12.)

_____

12.10 Some points to think about

a. How can you see where a subroutine starts in a program?
b. How does a function differ from a procedure?

12.11 Discussion on the points to think about

a. You cannot see the first line of a subroutine unless it is
   marked, for example by:

   REM subroutine...

b. A function is used wherever a variable might otherwise appear
   and gives a value just as a variable would. A procedure
   performs some operation more like a miniature program in its
   own right.

12.12 Discussion of activities

12.4 iii. The axes-drawing program, modified to work as a
procedure called by PROCaxes, is as follows:

```
   10 DEF PROCaxes
   20 LOCAL X,Y
   30 REM Draw x axis
   40 FOR Y = 80 TO 84 STEP 4
   50    MOVE 238,Y : DRAW 1200,Y
   60 NEXT Y
   70 REM
   80 REM Draw y axis
   90 FOR X = 234 TO 238 STEP 4
  100    MOVE X,80 : DRAW X,1000
  110 NEXT X
  120 ENDPROC
```

12.7 i. Sorting out the maximum of four values is probably best
done with simple comparisons of the following form:

```
 1000 DEF FNmax(a,b,c,d)
 1010 IF b>a THEN a=b
 1020 IF c>a THEN a=c
 1030 IF d>a THEN a=d
 1040 =a
```

12.7 iii. The error will be for a number that is too large. You will
find that the number of recursions allowed for a procedure depends

on the amount of memory available.

12.7 iv.

10 DEF FNcentigrade(F) = (F - 32)*5/9

12.9 ii. For this subroutine you need to make sure that the first time it is called, Fact is given the value N. We have done this in line 1020. Note that variables cannot be declared as local for subroutines; so check very carefully to make sure all variables in the subroutines occur nowhere else in the program. This subroutine can cope only with integers from 1 to 26.

```
1000 REM subroutine factorial
1010 REM returns with Fact = N!
1020 Visit = Visit + 1 : IF Visit = 1 THEN Fact = N
1030 IF N=1 THEN Visit = 0: RETURN
1040 N = N -1 : Fact = Fact * N :GOSUB 1000
1050 RETURN
```

Note the ending for this subroutine. The subroutine-calling mechanism keeps a careful count of the number of GOSUBs executed, and the line number following the GOSUB. It expects to find a corresponding number of RETURN statements. With this subroutine no RETURN statements are found until the value of N reaches 1. At this stage the line which said GOSUB would then have been 1040 and so the RETURN would return to 1050. Line 1050 says RETURN but the corresponding GOSUB was found on line 1040; so it will once again and repeatedly keep coming back to 1050 until from the final RETURN it will go back to the the statement following the GOSUB which started the whole process.

Checking bytes free

13 File handling

13.0 Introduction

A 'file' is a block of stored information. It may be a program, some numerical data, or a letter composed on a word processor package. It can be saved and retrieved by an identifying name. You have already recorded and loaded programs with a tape recorder and, as such, have created and used simple files. In this chapter we shall be considering the more sophisticated use of files, in particular how they can be manipulated by programs.

150

13.1 Disc versus cassette tape

Files can be held on discs as well as on cassette tapes. A disc is made of a magnetic medium which revolves many times a second in use. The information is written in lots of small sub packages at various places over the disc, and while the disc revolves, the computer keeps track of them and can almost instantaneously put them together into a unified whole. Alternatively, the computer can merely pick out and use various parts of the information from anywhere in the file. This type of access is termed 'random access'. With a cassette tape, on the other hand, reading normally has to start at the beginning and proceed in order to the end - which is termed 'serial access'.

With a disc system, once you have asked for a particular file, the reading typically starts in less than a second from pressing the return key and is complete in a matter of seconds, much faster than with tape. Also with a disc system you can read from more than one file at a time and need not start from the beginning. With a cassette system of a single tape recorder, you will only be able to read from one file at a time and will have to start from the beginning. Furthermore the disc system keeps a record of all the files on the disc and knows where to find any part of any one of them. The cassette system keeps no such record.

A disc system for the BBC Microcomputer costs ten to twenty times as much as a cassette recorder and is about as much as the simplest version of the computer itself (see Appendix). Most users will therefore decide to stick with a cassette recorder - and we would not like to suggest that some very useful file handling cannot be achieved with it. The point is that, as most of the statements for file handling are essentially designed for disc systems, you will only get the most out of a cassette system if you understand something about disc systems.

We will therefore describe file handling for a disc system although we will certainly emphasize where a cassette recorder is also appropriate. We felt that if we tried to tackle the subject the other way round, you might not appreciate why things are designed a particular way and so might not be able to use your own system to advantage.

13.2 Files as data stores

There is some similarity between a file and a block of DATA statements since both store information which can be retrieved. However, whereas DATA statements can only be read by the program to which they are attached, files can be read by any program. Also whereas DATA statements need to be typed in by a programmer, files can be created by the computer during execution of a program.

For all practical purposes, a program can create as many disc files as you specify and their lengths can be as long as you like provided they are within the storage capacity of the system. The same is true with cassette tape except that only one file can be in use at a time.

13.3 Writing to files

An analogy for a file system is a library, where each book is a file with its own unique name. The books can be large or small and - if the analogy is with a disc system - you need not start reading from the beginning unless you wish.

Before you can write a file, you must do the equivalent of supplying the front cover for the book. This is called 'opening out' the file and you do it by a line like one of the following, where # is called 'hash', and where C is a numerical variable by which you must refer to the file within the program:

          100 C = OPENOUT"file_name"
or
          100 C = OPENOUT A$

Once the file is opened out, you write data into it with a PRINT statement. The data may be numbers or strings which can be mixed in any fashion. By way of illustration, the following is an instruction to write data to the file C. The data includes a numerical value from an array, the number 567 and the strings "hello" and stock$:

          200 PRINT# C,A(I),567,"hello",STOCK$

You can carry on putting data into the file for as long as the program is running. Although the amount is eventually limited by the storage capacity of the system, this is rarely a limitation.

If you should happen to want to know how long the file has grown, you can request this information by means of the following lines which work with a disc sytem only:

          235 L = EXT# C
          240 PRINT "length of file =";L

This prints L, the length of the file in bytes. A 'byte' is the smallest cell of memory which can be separately addressed. Typically it can hold one character.

The file is only usable when it has had the equivalent of the back cover of the book put on. This is called 'closing' the file and may be performed by either of the following statements. The first closes a specific file C and the second closes all files:

          540 CLOSE# C

        540 CLOSE# 0

The following is an example program which will read some data from
DATA statements and write them out to a file named TRIAL1. The
first number in the data is the number of following pairs of items to
be read in:

```
   10 A = OPENOUT"TRIAL1"
   20 READ N
   30 PRINT# A,N
   40 FOR J = 1 TO N
   50    READ D,D$
   60    PRINT# A,D,D$
   70 NEXT J
   80 CLOSE# A
   90 PRINT "File writing complete" : END
 1000 DATA 4
 1010 DATA 345,"squirrel",4,"rabbit"
 1020 DATA 28,"cat",38,"canary"
```

When the OPENOUT statement is executed with a disc system, the
computer searches to see if a file of that name exists. If it does, the
computer opens it for more material to be written to the end of it.
If the file does not exist, the computer opens a new file with that
name. For a cassette system, the computer automatically starts a new
file, irrespective of whether one already exists.

13.4 Reading from files

In the same way as you can retrieve information from a book by
'dipping into' it, you can inform the system which file you wish to
access by 'opening into' it. You do this by naming the file with a
statement such as the following:

        230 F = OPENIN"file_name"
or
        230 File_num = OPENIN G$

Once again the computer provides the reference number by which it
refers to the file, and you provide the variable F and File_num to
hold the reference number. The value of F or File_num is now used
in the program as the reference number for this file - but once again
only for the duration of the current program. Reading data from the
file is achieved with the following slight variation of the INPUT
statement, where F is the variable holding the number of the file,
and the other variables are to be assigned values from the file:

        310 INPUT# F,NAME$,COST,X,Y,A$

The reading of data from the file normally starts at the beginning
and works through in strict order. So a value for NAME$ is the
first item that this INPUT statement takes in. The last is a value
for A$.

As with all INPUT statements, it is important for a string
variable to pick up the correct string and for a numerical variable to
be given only the right numerical value. If a string is read as the
value for a numerical variable, the value assigned will be
VAL(String$). It is just as important to know the order of the items
in the file as it is when reading from DATA statements.

By means of the following program, you could read back the data
from the program of the previous section which wrote a file:

```
100 B = OPENIN"TRIAL1"
110 INPUT# B,N
120 FOR J = 1 TO N
130    INPUT# B,M,M$ : PRINT M,M$
140 NEXT J
150 CLOSE#0
160 END
```

When line 100 is executed, the computer searches the disc for a file
with the supplied name. If it is found, it is opened at the beginning
for reading. Line 130 both reads in the data and prints it out on the
screen.

When any program using files comes to the end, the computer
should be told that it has finished with whatever files it was using.
This can be done with a statement like CLOSE#B, or alternatively
all files can be closed together with the one statement CLOSE#0.
CLOSE statements are the same irrespective of whether the files
were opened out for writing or opened into for accessing.

If you forget to close a file which was opened for writing, you
may lose data, as the end section may not have been recorded. If you
forget to close a file which was opened for reading, it is not as
serious. Nevertheless it is good program practice to close all files
when you have finished using them.

13.5 Activities

---

i. For this activity we will assume that you have a cassette tape
recorder rather than a disc system. Enter the program for writing a
file in section 13.3 and that for reading a file in 13.4. Now wind
your cassette tape on, by hand, beyond the leader to the beginning of
the recording medium. Set the recorder to record and run the
program so as to write the file, with the name TRIAL1, to tape.
When the tape has completed its run, stop it and rewind.

ii. Run the second program to read a file by entering GOTO 100.

Nothing will happen until you set your tape recorder to play. Is the correct data written on the screen?

iii. Why do you have to wait a little while before the data is written to the screen? (Section 13.10 deals with this point.)

13.6 Reading and writing byte by byte

The previous statements which allow you to write numbers and strings to files should satisfy most of your needs. However, should you require it, you can have more complete control of files if you are prepared to deal with information a byte at a time.

The byte is the smallest quantity of information that it is normally useful to consider. It can hold individual characters or codes. Normally numbers and strings are written several bytes at a time. When a file is written using the PRINT statement, all strings are recorded as character codes, finishing with a return character. (Yes! There is an ASCII code for return; it is recorded at the end of every string.) Numbers are written as five byte binary numbers.

It is possible to write a byte at a time. The file needs to be opened in the normal way, for example:

        10 N = OPENOUT"trial"

Then a byte can be written to the end of the file by means of lines like the following, where the file number is contained by either N or Accounts_file and the byte is 13 or P respectively:

        140 BPUT# N,13
or
        140 BPUT# Accounts_file,P

A byte can only hold the code for one ASCII character or any other 8 bit binary number - which in everyday language means a number between 0 and 255. If the value that the program tries to write is greater than 255, the computer considers the number as broken down into bytes and it takes the least significant byte. Once you have written to a file in the byte mode, it will not be readable with the normal INPUT unless you have taken great care to use the same format as the PRINT# statement for files. Of course if you only want the byte mode for reading back, this is no problem.

To read a file a byte at a time, the file needs to have been opened in the normal way with, for example, F=OPENIN"finance". The following lines each read in a single byte:

        180 G = BGET# N

or
        180 P = BGET# Accounts_file

These lines are exactly equivalent to the previous byte-writing lines and so can retrieve the same data. The necessity for matching the method of reading to that of writing cannot be too strongly emphasized.

The byte mode gives a great deal of control but allows for more possibilities of error. You should not use it until you are fully competent at the simpler file handling operations. If you want the file to be available for subsequent reading using INPUT, you should have studied the organization of files very carefully. The way in which numerical values and strings are written should be followed exactly for anything other than byte reading.

While a file is being read, it is important for the computer to keep track of where it is in the file, so that the next time the program asks for some data, it knows where to get it. The computer achieves this by means of what is termed a 'pointer', which is a record of the position in the file at which the next read will occur. In the byte mode you have access to this pointer and can move it around. This means that you do not have to read the file from the beginning, and indeed, if you have a disc system, you can even read it backwards!

For a disc system the pointer can be moved using PTR which is the name of a variable with a value equal to the current pointer position on the file. It can be used like a normal variable in that it can be given a value. The following lines show an application of its use to move the pointer on by 32 bytes within a file F already opened for reading:

        230 PTR#F = PTR#F + 32

Reading a file backwards byte by byte may seem a little odd but is entirely feasible using the following simple program:

        10 F = OPENIN"Accounts_file"
        20 FOR K = EXT#A -1 TO 0 STEP -1
        30   PTR#F = K
        40   PRINT BGET#F;
        50 NEXT K
        60 CLOSE#K
        70 END

This program cannot of course run with a cassette system which is made purely for reading forwards in a serial fashion. You should not use the byte pointer for random access to a file unless you have a disc based system.

You may test to see if the end of a file has been reached while reading with the EOF function. The letters stand for End Of File.

EOF is used in IF . . THEN and REPEAT . . UNTIL loops and is equivalent to a comparison which is not true until the end of the file. The test could be written as follows:

```
        150 IF EOF#N THEN END
or
        280 IF NOT EOF#A THEN 50
or
        140 REPEAT
        . . . . .
        . . . . .
        . . . . .
        230 UNTIL EOF#N
```

13.7 Activities

---

i. Just to show that it is possible, we will have an activity on byte writing using a cassette tape recorder. First enter the following program to record two bytes separated by 130 zeroes:

```
        10 F = OPENOUT"TRIAL2"
        20 BPUT#F,ASC("A")
        30 FOR J=1 TO 130 : BPUT #F,0 : NEXT J
        40 BPUT#F,ASC("B")
        50 CLOSE#F
        60 END
```

Wind to the start of the cassette and set your tape recorder to record. Then run the program.

ii. Now wind the tape back to the start and enter the following program to read the file TRIAL2 and print the contents on the screen.

```
        10 F=OPENIN"TRIAL2"
        20 PRINT"Byte pointer =";PTR#F
        30 REPEAT
        40    Y$ = CHR$(BGET#F)
        50    PRINT Y$;
        60 UNTIL EOF# F
        70 PRINT"Byte pointer =";PTR#F
        80 END
```

With a disc system the byte pointer printed by line 70 will show that 132 bytes have been read in. The pointer does not work with a cassette tape system. Do you see that only the characters A and B are printed on the screen? Can you explain this? (See section

13.10.)

13.8 Some points to think about

a. Why is it necessary to open files for writing as nothing seems to need doing before writing starts?
b. Even if the OPENOUT statement is necessary before starting to write to a file, no CLOSE might seem to be, if no more writing is to take place. Why will you have trouble if you leave off the CLOSE statement?
c. If you leave off the CLOSE statement will anything be written to the file?

13.9 Discussion on the points to think about

a. The system needs to know whether it is to open a new file or add to an old one. The only way it can know the difference is if you declare the file for opening first. It can then search to see if this file exists or not. For a cassette system it is always assumed that a file to be written to is a new one.
b. Each file is written in blocks of a fixed length. Thus while a program is writing characters to a file, the operating system will hold these in a buffer until sufficient have accumulated to make up the standard number it writes out. The whole block is then written in one go. When the CLOSE statement is executed this is an instruction to the operating system to write out the rest of its buffer without waiting for it to be filled up. It does so by filling the remaining spaces in the buffer with nulls (0). Thus the omission of CLOSE prevents the last block from being written out.
c. If CLOSE is omitted, only the last block of the file is not written out. All the rest of the file is recorded.

13.10 Discussion of activities

13.5 iii. The program should search the tape for a file called TRIAL1, and the program should read nothing from the tape until such a file name is found.

If you record many files on the same tape you may have to wait a long time for the correct one to be found. If the tape was started beyond the position where the name of the file was recorded, the subsequent data would not be read in.

13.7 ii. A zero is known as a null character. It does nothing if a program tries to print it, for instance. Thus this program will only print the characters for A and B. The zero or null bytes were still written to the file and, with a disc system, the byte pointer will show their presence.

RAM *storage*

14 Programmable characters and sound

14.0 Introduction

When you come to program games, you will probably want a character
or figure that is not one of the standard keyboard set - perhaps a
pin-man, a football or a space invader. Fortunately the BBC

Microcomputer allows you to define characters to your own design. It also offers another facility which is particularly useful for games: sound effects. In this, its provision is rather exceptional. Although many computers emit simple notes, these tend to sound rather 'electronic'. They rely on simply turning the notes on and off, in contrast to real musical instruments whose sounds build up and decay in a way characteristic of the type of instrument. The BBC Microcomputer is exceptional in allowing the programmer to control these aspects. Consequently its sound is much more pleasing and makes games programs more realistic. However, programming the sound can be extremely complicated. We merely give an introduction - and even of this you may choose to omit the end sections.

14.1 Principles of defining new characters

Each screen character is made up of dots within a matrix eight dots high and eight dots wide. Although it is possible to define a figure as large as you like by putting characters together, we shall start by looking at how to define a single character within an 8 by 8 matrix. This consists of programming some of the sixty-four dots to light up in the foreground colour and the others in the background colour. VDU 23 allows this for all modes other than mode 7.

The first step in evaluating these numbers is to sketch a picture of the character to be programmed. Let us illustrate by supposing that we wish to draw a little man. We can sketch him within an eight by eight matrix as shown in figure 14.1.

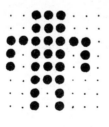

fig 14.1

We can send this picture to the computer by means of binary numbers. The set of binary numbers in Table 14.1 traces out the same picture. Look closely and you will see that the 0's represent the dots and the 1's represent the blobs. The equivalent ordinary number is inside a bracket after each binary number. It is these ordinary (base 10) numbers that we send to the computer to define the character.

```
00111000  (=56)
00111000  (=56)
11111110  (=254)
10111010  (=186)
10111010  (=186)
00111000  (=56)
00101000  (=40)
00101000  (=40)
```

Table 14.1

Any character with an ASCII code between 32 and 255 (with the exception of 127) may have its appearance reprogrammed. For example, to program the character whose ASCII code is 32 to appear as the little man would require a program line like the following. The VDU 23 statement announces that the next number is the ASCII code for a character which is to be reprogrammed, and the following eight numbers are the ordinary number equivalents of the binary numbers as shown in Table 14.1. The 1's define the foreground while the 0's define the background:

100 VDU 23,32,56,56,254,186,186,56,40,40

When characters are redefined, the extra information is held in memory. On the BBC Microcomputer, sufficient space is available for the thirty-two characters with ASCII codes from 224 to 255. For other ASCII codes, the extra space has to be found by altering the position at which the current program is stored. We will not go into this, but will assume that you will be redefining only characters with ASCII codes from 224 to 255.

14.2 Defining composite figures

In practice our little man is too small to be recognized easily on the screen. This often happens with characters within a single eight by eight matrix. Fortunately we can make composite figures by joining characters. The characters can be joined next to each other or on top of each other or both.

For example we can draw a more recognizable little man as a composite figure using four characters, each within an eight by eight matrix, as shown in Table 14.2. There are two rows, each with two 8 bit binary numbers. To print him, we have to redefine four characters and then print them as a block: two together on one line with the second pair directly underneath on the next line. Let us choose the characters corresponding to codes 224,225,226 and 227. We will print the first two together on one line with PRINT CHR$(224);CHR$(225) and will use VDU 5 to print at a graphics position. The first two sections of our man might be located with the program:

```
100 VDU 5     : REM text at graphics locations
110 MOVE X,Y  : REM location of man
120 PRINT CHR$(224);CHR$(225)
```

0000000100000000	(=1,0)
0000110001100000	(=12,96)
0000010001000000	(=4,64)
0000001110000000	(=3,128)
0000000110000000	(=1,128)
0000001110000000	(=3,128)
0000111101100000	(=15,96)
0001101100110000	(=27,48)
1111001101100000	(=241,96)
0000001100000000	(=3,0)
0000011011000000	(=6,192)
0001100011000000	(=24,192)
0011000011000000	(=48,192)
0011000000110000	(=48,48)
0011000000111000	(=48,56)
1100000000000000	(=192,0)

Table 14.2

The bottom two characters for the man need to be printed immediately below the first two. Fortunately there are always 32 lines displayed on the screen and so the shift in the y coordinate to move to the next line is always also 32 (1024/32 =32). To print out the bottom half of the man requires the extra two lines:

```
130 MOVE X,Y-32
140 PRINT CHR$(226);CHR$(227)
```

It is much quicker to print the man using a single string and what are known as 'line feed' characters and 'backspace' characters. The line feed character CHR$(10) moves the cursor down vertically by one line and the backspace character CHR$(8) moves it one space backwards. These are incorporated into the following string:

```
120 man$ = CHR$(224)+CHR$(225)+CHR$(10)+CHR$(8)
    +CHR$(8)+CHR$(226)+CHR$(227)
```

One line feed plus two backspaces brings us from the start of the top half of the man to the start of the bottom half. The printing is achieved with the following line:

```
130 PRINT man$
```

14.3 Activities

---

i. Define the character corresponding to ASCII 224, using the
following line:

    VDU 23,224,56,56,254,186,56,40,40

Print it using:

    PRINT CHR$(224)

Do you get a tiny man? Do you agree that it is too small for
practical purposes?

ii. Redefine characters 224 to 227 and produce a larger man with the
following short program:

```
10 VDU 23,224,1,12,4,3,1,3,15,27
20 VDU 23,225,0,96,64,128,128,128,96,48
30 VDU 23,226,241,3,6,24,48,48,48,192
40 VDU 23,227,96,0,192,192,192,48,56,0
50 PRINT CHR$(224)+CHR$(225)+CHR$(10)+CHR$(8)
   +CHR$(8)+CHR$(226)+CHR$(227)
60 END
```

Have you produced a picture of a man?

14.4 Moving composite figures

The following program lines set up graphics mode 5, define the
characters for the parts of the man and define a procedure called
PROCman(X,Y) which draws the man at position X,Y:

```
10 MODE5 : GCOL 0,2 : REM draw in colour 2
20 VDU 5  : REM text printed at graphics position
30 REM define man characters 224,225,226,227
40 VDU 23,224,1,12,4,3,1,3,15,27
50 VDU 23,225,0,96,64,128,128,128,96,48
60 VDU 23,226,241,3,6,24,48,48,48,192
70 VDU 23,227,96,0,192,192,192,48,56,0
80 REM jump round multi-line procedure
90 GOTO 140
100 DEF PROCman(X,Y)
110 MOVE X,Y    : PRINT CHR$(224);CHR$(225)
120 MOVE X,Y-32 : PRINT CHR$(226);CHR$(227)
130 ENDPROC
```

140 . . . .

Lines from 140 onwards may draw the man at any designated position merely by calling on the procedure. Thus to move him across the screen from right to left could be achieved with a simple REPEAT . . UNTIL loop which also prints him. After a delay he is rubbed out again before being moved on.

With graphics mode 5 there are four colours. We shall make use of the following colour scheme to display the man, not only moving across the screen, but also disappearing behind various coloured objects.

    0 = yellow background
    1 = man = black
    2 = green = objects for man to pass behind
    3 = green (for the reason, see below)

The background is made yellow by redefining the background colour 0 using the statement VDU19,0,3;0; in line 160. The cactus is drawn on the screen by lines 190 to 210. All subsequent drawing is set by GCOL3,1 in line 230 to the EOR operation. The binary part of the number representing the colour of any area of the screen takes the following form:

    colour number = binary 00 for background
    colour number = binary 01 for man
    colour number = binary 10 for cactus object

The first binary digit indicates whether the screen point is background (0) or cactus (1). The second binary digit indicates the presence or otherwise of the man. Note the new colour definitions which we are going to set up. They are:

    binary 00 = yellow (background)
    binary 01 = black (man on background)
    binary 10 = green (cactus)
    binary 11 = green (man and cactus together)

Since we have arranged that the colour when the man crosses the cactus is the same as that of the cactus itself, the man will seem to disappear as he crosses the cactus. He will thus seem to walk behind it. As he is written to the screen using logical EOR then the information as to whether he is crossing background or cactus is not lost. At the same time the use of EOR means that if he is written to the same spot a second time, the area is returned to its original colour.

The complete program is made from lines 10 to 130, together with the following. It draws a yellow background, a green cactus and a little man moving across the screen.

```
140 REM now define colours, 0=yellow, 1=black
150 REM 2=green, 3=green
160 VDU 19,0,3;0; : VDU 19,1,0;0; : VDU 19,3,2;0;
    : VDU 19,2,2;0;
170 REM draw a cactus
180 RESTORE 1000
190 FOR P=1 TO 18
200    READ M,x,y : PLOT M,x,y
210 NEXT P
220 REM set up EOR of man's colour
230 GCOL3,1
240 REM
250 REM now move man continuously across screen
260 X=1279 : Y=460
270 REPEAT
280    PROCman(X,Y) : REM draw man
290    FOR I=1 TO 50 : NEXT I
300    PROCman(X,Y) : REM rub man out
310    X=X-8
320 UNTIL X < 0
330 GOTO 260
1000 DATA 68,690,400,68,600,400,85,690,430
1010 DATA 85,600,430,68,600,600,85,630,430
1020 DATA 85,630,600,68,700,300,68,740,300
1030 DATA 86,700,710,85,740,710,68,740,420
1040 DATA 68,830,420,85,740,450,85,830,450
1050 DATA 68,830,670,85,800,450,85,800,670
```

14.5 Activities

---

i. Enter and run the complete program which makes the man seem to walk behind the cactus. Does it behave as you expect?

ii. Note that when the man has crossed the screen once, his image remains on the left of the screen. Why does this happen? Modify the program so as to eliminate it.

iii. If you have an expanded computer, try modifying the program to run in mode 2. Make the man appear to move in front of some objects and behind others. (The colour numbers from 0 to 15 mean you have four binary bits instead of two to play with.)

14.6 Describing sound

The BBC Microcomputer contains a sound generator and a small loudspeaker. It emits sound when the SOUND statement is executed. This statement allows you to control the pitch, the quality, the loudness and the duration of the sound. In this section, we shall describe what these terms mean.

You have probably seen sound represented on an oscilloscope and realize that it is a vibration. The rate of vibration is known as the 'frequency'. The faster the vibration, the higher the frequency and the higher the pitch of the note.

When the waveform of the sound is regular as shown in figure 14.2, the note is said to be 'pure'. The greatest displacement is described as the 'amplitude'. The greater the amplitude, the greater the intensity and the louder the sound.

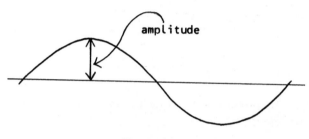

fig 14.2

When the waveform is less regular, but the frequency is still constant, as shown in figure 14.3, the sound is described as containing 'harmonics'. Notes of the same pitch from different musical instruments sound different because of their differing harmonics. They are also described as being of different 'quality'. It is the harmonics that add the pleasing quality to a note.

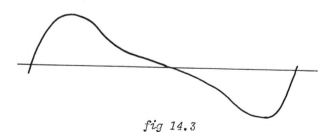

fig 14.3

The 'envelope' is a useful term for describing a more complicated waveform. In figure 14.4 it is indicated by the dotted line.

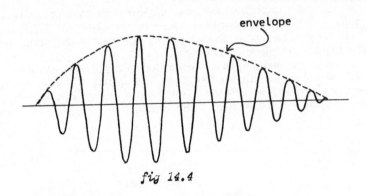

fig 14.4

A sound is described as 'noise' when there is no discernable pattern to its waveform.

14.7 The simple SOUND statement

In its simplest form the SOUND statement is given by:

SOUND channel, amplitude, pitch, duration

We shall now explain 'channel'. The BBC Microcomputer can provide three pure notes of different frequencies and a noise. Each is available on what is called a channel. Channels 1, 2 and 3 give the pure notes and channel 0 gives the noise - which can sound like a hiss or a gunshot depending on how long it lasts. So the first number in the SOUND statement must be between 0 and 3.

The second number in the SOUND statement represents amplitude, and must be between 0 and -15: 0 for silence and -15 for the maximum loudness. (We will wait until later to discuss the significance of the negative sign.)

The third number in the SOUND statement concerns pitch. It has to be specified in a unit called the 'quarter semitone'. You may know from music that there are are twelve semitones to an octave, i.e. adding 12 semitones changes a note to one an octave higher up the scale. For the SOUND statement - requiring quarter semitones - you would have to add 48 to the pitch number for an octave change. The lowest available note, given by 0, produces the A below middle C on the musical scale. The SOUND statement accepts any number between 0 and 255 for pitch. This covers 64 semitones or just over five octaves.

'Duration' is the time for which the note lasts. The SOUND statement requires it to be specified in hundredths of a second, and accepts any number between 1 and 254. So 50 represents a duration of half a second and 100 represents a duration of one second.

We shall now illustrate substituting into the SOUND statement. The following produces a sound on the first pure note channel (given by 1) with maximum amplitude (given by -15) with the lowest pitch available (given by 0) and of duration 1 second (given by 100):

```
10 SOUND 1,-15,0,100
```

The following statements produce a series of notes on the same channel, namely channel 1, with maximum amplitude, random pitch and length 0.2 seconds:

```
10 SOUND 1,-15,RND(254),20
20 GOTO 10
```

You can produce chords using all three channels. For example A major would require the notes A, C and E to be sounded together. You could define them with the following three lines which are executed almost simultaneously:

```
10 SOUND 1,-15,0,50
20 SOUND 2,-15,12,50
30 SOUND 3,-15,28,50
```

Some chords may not sound particularly pleasing. This is due to the sensitivity of the ear and the limitations of the chips used in the sound synthesis. Unfortunately there is nothing that you can do about it.

14.8 Activities

---

i. The following program plays a series of notes of random pitch on each of the three pure note channels in turn. The sound is rather jumbled and you may like to compare it later with a more ordered sound. (If so, save the program.) Enter and run the program.

```
10 FOR J%=1 TO 30
20    channel% = channel%+1 : IF channel%=4
     THEN channel%=1
30    SOUND channel%,-15,RND(254),30
40 NEXT J%
50 END
```

ii. The following program displays the notes being sent from BASIC to the operating system. Examine the listing. Then enter and run the program. Watch the numbers as they are written to the screen and compare this with the emission of the corresponding sound. (We analyse this in the next section.)

```
10 FOR J%=1 TO 20
20    channel%=channel%+1 : IF channel%=4
      THEN channel%=1
30    pitch%=RND(254)
40    SOUND channel%,-15,pitch%,20
50    PRINT "Loop ";J%;" pitch = ";pitch%
60 NEXT J%
70 PRINT "program has already finished running!!"
80 END
```

14.9 Queues

The second program of the previous activities rapidly prints up sixteen numbers, followed by a message indicating its completion. Yet a succession of notes still sound for some time! We shall now explain this.

When two notes are sent to the same channel, the second has to wait until the first has finished sounding. Meanwhile it has to be remembered. The computer can remember up to four notes at a time for each channel. It can accept them just as rapidly as they are sent, but any more than four get held up. They are then said to be in a 'queue'. It is the notes in the queue that sound after the program has finished executing.

14.10 The complete SOUND statement

At times you may want to override a queue and force a note to be played immediately. You may also want to sound certain notes simultaneously. All this and more is controlled by the complete SOUND statement. Its form is as follows:

SOUND &HSFC,amplitude/envelope,pitch,duration

Incidentally the & indicates that the number which follows is in 'hexadecimal' - which means that it is to base sixteen - but this need not concern you.

We shall now explain the meanings of H, S, F and C. You will probably find it easiest if we do so in reverse order.

C is the channel, with which you are already familiar. It can have a value between 0 and 3.

F stands for Flush the queue. It can be either 0 or 1. If you leave it out, 0 is assumed and the sound-generation takes place as described above. If F=1 then notes still waiting to be sounded on channel C are removed from the queue, and the note which is already sounding is cut off. This is useful when you want a sound to come out immediately you execute the sound statement.

S gives the number of notes that are to be sounded together; it can take a value of 0, 1, 2 or 3. If S = 0, no notes are sounded together, so a note is emitted according to its turn in the queue. If S = 1, one note is held up, so that two are sounded together; if S = 2, two notes are held up, so that three are sounded together; and if S = 3, three notes are held up, so that four notes are sounded together. S as 1, 2 or 3 enables you to program chords, which tend to give a more pleasing sound than single notes.

The following three lines of program illustrate the use of S in the complete SOUND statement. Since S = 2, the notes are emitted as a chord:

```
10 SOUND &0201,-15,0,20
20 SOUND &0202,-15,4,20
30 SOUND &0203,-15,8,20
```

H can have a value of 0 or 1. You will normally want H as 0, which corresponds to the simple SOUND statement. A note with H = 1 is a 'dummy' note in that it does not itself sound. 1 allows the after effects of a previous note to be maintained - but you will understand this more when we discuss the ENVELOPE statement in section 14.12.

Apart from the &HSFC there is another difference between the simple and complete form of the SOUND statement. In the complete form amplitude/envelope replaces just amplitude. Whereas amplitude can have a value between 0 and -15, envelope can have a value between 1 and 4 - but more of this in section 14.12.

14.11 Activities

The following program sounds notes first without a simultaneous start and then with synchronism. We have used a random number for the pitch; so the chords will not sound musically correct.

```
10 PRINT "This is non-simultaneous!"
20 FOR J%=1 TO 3
30    SOUND J%,-15,RND(254),30
40    FOR I=1 TO 1000 : NEXT I
50 NEXT J%
60 REM wait for notes to die
70 FOR I = 1 TO 3000 : NEXT I
80 REM now the chord
```

```
 90 PRINT "NOW SIMULTANEOUS!"
100 FOR J%=1 TO 3
110    SOUND &200+J%,-15,RND(254),30
120    FOR I=1 TO 1000 : NEXT I
130 NEXT J%
140 FOR I = 1 TO 3000 : NEXT I
150 GOTO 10
```

Run the program and note the difference between the two types of chord. Can you detect the crisper starting sound for the chords produced by the second half of the program?

14.12 The ENVELOPE statement

The BBC Microcomputer can store up to 4 envelopes at any one time. You can define them yourself using the ENVELOPE statement and identify them by values of N from 1 to 4. For example, you can define envelope 1 so that it mimics the sharp attacking clash of a cymbal or, say, envelope 2 so that it is similar to the more gentle whisper of a flute. The following is the general form of the ENVELOPE statement, where N is the envelope number:

```
10 ENVELOPE N,S,  PS1,PS2,PS3,NS1,NS2,NS3,
       AR,DR,SR,RR,PL,SL
```

The spaces provide a marker between the various parts of the statement. We recommend that you always include them so that you can easily check that you have the correct number of values. There should be 14 in all.

We shall now discuss the meanings and values of the terms in the ENVELOPE statement. They are summarized in Table 14.3.

SYMBOL	NAME	RANGE
N	envelope number	1 to 4
S	duration	0 to 255
PS1,2,3	pitch step	-128 to +127
NS1,2,3	number of steps	0 to 255
AR	attack rate	1 to 127
DR	decay rate	-127 to +127
SR	sustain rate	0 to -128
RR	release rate	0 to -128
PL	peak level	0 to 126
SL	sustain level	0 to 126

Table 14.3

S defines the duration of the various features. If S=0, the
duration is one hundredth of a second. If S=1, it is two hundredths.
If S=2, it is three hundredths and so on.

The BBC Microcomputer takes an envelope as being defined in
terms of four sections, bounded by straight lines as shown in fig
14.5. Six constants define the four slopes and two fixed amplitudes.
These constants comprise six of the terms in the ENVELOPE
statement.

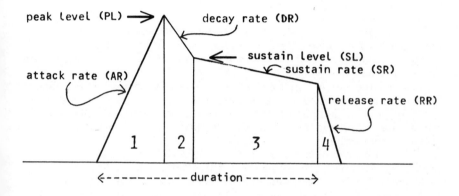

fig 14.5 :   sections of envelope

The rate at which the amplitude of the note develops is termed
the 'attack rate' and is represented by AR. It is given in steps per
unit time interval - which is dictated by S.

The maximum value of the amplitude at the end of the attack
period is called the 'peak level' and is represented by PL. With
AR=50 and PL=150 there would have to be 3 steps for the attack
amplitude to go from 0 to 150. The time per step is dictated by S.
If this were 1, say, there would be 2 hundredths of a second per
step. This would give a time for the attack of 3 times 2, i.e. 6
hundredths of a second.

We will deal only with the amplitude decaying down to a second
set level called the 'sustain level', represented by SL. The rate of
decay from the peak level to the sustain level is similarly
controlled by the 'decay rate' DR. With the sustain level SL less
than the peak level PL, the decay rate DR has to be negative.

The rate at which the portion SR falls off is similarly dictated
by the value given to SR. You have to assign it a negative value.

The duration of the note as defined in the SOUND statement
dictates the length of the note from its start to the end of the slope

SR. At the end of this period, the note goes into the last phase,
labelled RR for 'release rate'. You only hear this note if no new one
follows it, in which case the rate of fall of amplitude is dictated by
the value you assign to RR. If a new note does immediately follow
the current one, the phase RR is cut off and the new note starts to
sound.

Summarizing so far, a typical envelope could be defined by the
line:

```
10 ENVELOPE 1,0,  0,0,0,0,0,0,
   126,-4,0,-2,126,95
```

It defines envelope 1 with time interval the minimum of one
hundredth of a second. The envelope has an attack which goes up in
steps of 126 to a level of 126 and thus in one jump. The decay rate
is -4 and has to cause a drop from 126 to 95, a difference of 31
which in steps of 4 will take 8 steps. The sustain rate is 0 and thus
the amplitude remains constant until the time dictated by the value
of the duration in the SOUND statement. The note will then fall off
at a rate of -2 per step until the amplitude is zero provided no
further note follows.

The six central numbers in the ENVELOPE statement provide
extra control over the frequency of the note. They allow the
frequency to be varied with time in a manner similar to that of
amplitude. The numbers come in three pairs, each consisting of a
'pitch step' PS and a 'number of steps' NS: PS1 and NS1, PS2 and
NS2 etc. These dictate that the frequency should vary from the
start of the note in steps of size PS1,2 or 3 for a number of steps
given by the corresponding NS1,2 or 3. The step size is defined in
terms of the quarter semitone. The corresponding NS1,2 or 3 sets
the number of steps over which the frequency is to be varied. Thus
PS1=2 and NS1=10 would dictate that the frequency should be
increased for 10 steps each occupying the time set by S and each
step corresponding to 2 quarter semitones. Thus the overall effect
would be a change of frequency of 20 quarter semitones in a time of
10 units set by S. The three pairs of numbers in the frequency
section of the ENVELOPE statement allow the change of frequency
with time to have three parts to it.

To give full justice to the SOUND and ENVELOPE statements
would require a complete book - but to illustrate something of the
variety of the programmable sound, we now give some programs.

The following program will produce a 'laser gun' type of sound:

```
10 ENVELOPE 1,1,  100,0,-3,15,1,50,
   126,-1,0,-5,126,126
20 SOUND &11,1,55,6
30 TIME=0
40 IF TIME<300 THEN 40
50 SOUND &12,1,52,6
60 IF TIME<600 THEN 60
```

```
70 SOUND &13,1,50,6
80 END
```

The following program gives an effect rather like a gunfight:

```
10 FOR J%=1 TO 20
20 ENVELOPE 1,1, 0,0,0,0,0,0,  126,-1,0,-3,126,126
30 SOUND &10,1,3+RND(3),2
40 FOR I%=0 TO 300 + RND(2000) : NEXT I%
50 NEXT J%
60 END
```

The following program plays a rather nice tune:

```
10 ENVELOPE 1,1,  0,0,0,0,0,0,  126,-4,0,-2,126,95
20 DIM E%(20),N%(51) : EP%=0
30 N%(0)=0 : N%(1)=3 : N%(2)=7 : N%(3)=10
40 FOR I%=1 TO 4
50    FOR J%=0 TO 3
60       N%(J%+I%*4)=N%(J%)+I%*12
70    NEXT J%
80 NEXT I%
90 K%=0 : C%=(RND(4)-1)*4 : NL%=2 : D%=5 : X%=15
100 FOR I%=0 TO 600
110    IF I%MOD8=0 THEN K%=K%EOR5
120    IF I%MOD1=0 THEN R%=RND(2)
130    REPEAT
140       A%=RND(7)-4
150       UNTIL A%<>0 AND C%+A%<=19 AND C%+A%>=0
160    EP%=(EP%+1)MOD20 : E%(EP%)=N%(C%+A%) : C%=C%+A%
170    PROCwait(X%*R%)
180    SOUND1,1,(Fnpitch(1)+K%)*4,D%
190    PROCwait(X%)
200    SOUND2,1,(FNpitch(2)+K%)*4,D%
210    PROCwait(X%*(3-R%))
220    SOUND3,1,(FNpitch(3)+K%)*4,D%
230 NEXT
240 DEF FNpitch(Z%)=E%((EP%+NL%*(Z%-1))MOD20)
250 DEF PROCwait(W%) : NOW=TIME : REPEAT UNTIL
   TIME-NOW>W% : ENDPROC
260 END
```

14.13 Some points to think about

a. How could an image of a man be made to move its arms and
   legs while walking across the screen?
b. How could the image of the man be reversed so that he could
   walk first to the left and then to the right while always facing
   where he is going?

c.   How could the colours be redefined so that the little man's
     image could move behind some objects and in front of others?

14.14 Discussion on the points to think about

a.   If three separate images showing different poses of a little man
     are defined within the character set, the use of each in turn,
     while he is moved across the screen, can provide a realistic
     impression of walking.
b.   Reversing the images of the man would probably best be done
     using two versions of his image, stored in different character
     definitions. An alternative is to redefine the character each
     time the man's image is reversed.
c.   Using only four colours in mode 5, it would be impossible to
     make an image move both in front of and behind objects
     without redefining the composite colour of the image and object
     in the program. Such a redefinition can of course be made at
     any time. In mode 2 with sixteen colours available, many
     sophisticated effects are possible and it would be simple to
     define the composite colours of an object, logically ORed with
     the image to give whatever effect is required.

Where now?

Now that you have learnt about BASIC and the BBC
Microcomputer's facilities you will probably want to capitalize on
them. Where and how you do it will depend on the direction in which
you want to extend your computing expertise.

If you are a hobbyist, you will certainly find it valuable to
contact one of your local Computer Clubs or User Groups. A good
way is to visit Computer Shows where clubs and groups usually run
stands. Another way is to look in the national computer magazines.
They often publish useful addresses under such headings as Network
News, Feedback, Direct Access, Diary Dates, etc. In particular
Personal Computer World keeps an index of Computer User Groups
and Clubs. It publishes updates frequently and the complete list
several times a year.

If you want to develop your computing for professional or
business purposes, we suggest that you also contact your local club
or group. Members usually come from a variety of occupations and
backgrounds and will have quite a lot of information about what is
going on in your area. They will be able to advise you.

If you want to develop the educational aspects of computing, we
suggest the Microelectronics Education Programme (MEP). It
operates through a network of Regional Information Centres. For
details, contact:

> MEP
> Cheviot House
> Coach Lane Campus
> Newcastle-upon-Tyne NE6 7XA

Beebug is an independent association especially for users of the
BBC Microcomputer. Membership costs £4.50 for half a year and
£8.50 for a full year. For further information, contact:

> Beebug
> PO Box 50
> St Albans
> Herts

The BBC publish the following address for details of materials
available in connection with the BBC Computer Literacy Project. (A
12 by 9 inch stamped addressed envelope should accompany
enquiries.)

> Broadcasting Support Services
> P O Box 7
> London W3 6XJ

Peripherals

(The following information was current at the time of going to press.)

The BBC Microcomputer and its peripherals are available from:

> BBC Microcomputer System
> 14 Station Road
> Kettering
> Northamptonshire NN15 7HE

Prices include VAT at 15%; some prices are still to be announced (TBA).

The simplest model of the microcomputer

The simplest model of the microcomputer is known as Model A. It has 16K of RAM and offers graphics modes 4 to 7. It allows saving and retrieval with a cassette-tape system but not a disc system. It can be expanded to the Model B system.

Model A (ANA 01): £299.00

The expanded model of the microcomputer

The expanded model of the microcomputer is known as Model B. It has 32K of RAM and offers all the graphics modes, i.e. modes 0 to 7. It allows saving and retrieval with a cassette-tape system, and also accommodates a disc interface, disc drives and games paddles (see below).

Model B (ANB 01): £399.00

Econet Interface

An Econet interface allows a number of the microcomputers to be connected together in a ring with a printer and discs. Teachers will probably find this facility particularly useful in the classroom. The facility is available, at extra cost, with either model of the microcomputer.

Model A + Econet Interface (ANA 02): £263.00
Model B + Econet Interface (ANB 02): £446.00

Disc interface

A disc interface allows saving and retrieval on disc. It is available only for model B.

Model B + Disc Interface (ANB 03): £469.00
Model B + Disc and Econet Interface: £516.00

Second processor

An 8 bit second processor provides another complete set of 64K of RAM. With it the system behaves rather like a terminal and computer. The computer has a full 64K of memory and the terminal is itself intelligent with some memory storage. Two 8 bit processors are available: a Z80 and a 6502. The former allows use under CP/M for a disc system. A 16 bit processor is also available. It has 128K of memory. The operation of 16 bit processors is normally faster than 8 bit processors, and they normally have a more sophisticated set of instructions - resulting in a more powerful system.

Second processor - 6502 (ANC 01): TBA
Second processor - Z80 (ANC 02): TBA
Second processor - 16 bit (ANC 03) TBA

Disc drives

A single disc drive (100K) and a dual disc drive (800K) are available. The former might be rather short of memory for some purposes; the latter enables back-up copies to be made.

Single disc drive (AND 01): £265.00
Dual disc drive (AND 02): TBA

Teletext receiver

A teletext system can download programs from television, i.e. it can put them directly into the microcomputer without your having to type them out.

Teletext receiver (ANE 01): £166.00

Prestel receiver

A Prestel receiver allows access to the Prestel system and its pages of information with the computer acting as a terminal.

Prestel receiver (ANE 02): £103.50

Games paddles

Games paddles are levers for controlling play in games. For many types of games, this is superior than merely using the keyboard. Games paddles are supplied in pairs.

Games paddles (ANH 01): £13.00 per pair

Monitors

Monitors provide a better resolution than televisions and do not need tuning.

12" black and white monitor (ANF 01): £104.54
14" colour monitor (ANF 02): £287.50

Other peripherals

5 DIN to 25 way D Type serial cable (ANG 02): £9.50
Centronics-type printer cable (ANG 04): £18.40

Glossary

This is an overview of BASIC terms. For a fuller description, see the User Guide.

ABS   absolute value
ABS(p), ABS(a-b) or ABSp turns a negative value of p into a positive one of the same magnitude, but leaves a positive value of p or a-b unchanged.

ACS   arc-cosine
ACS(p) or ACSp gives the angle in radians whose cosine is p.

ADVAL   analogue to digital converter value
ADVAL(p), ADVALp or ADVAL3 gives the most recent value from the 12 bit analogue to digital channel p.

AND
AND is a Boolean operation between the binary version of two integer numbers. Its usage is similar to everyday English, as for example within IF . . THEN statements: IF A=B AND C<>D THEN . .

ASC   American Standard Code (ASCII)
ASC("s") gives the ASCII code for the first character of the string "s". If there are no characters in the string, it gives -1. Other examples are ASC(A$), ASCA$ and ASC"hello" which is same as ASC"h".

ASN   arc-sine
ASN(p) or ASNp gives the angle in radians whose sine is p.

ATN   arc-tangent
ATN(p) or ATNp gives the angle in radians whose tangent is p.

AUTO   automatic
AUTO allows program lines to be entered without their line numbers being typed first. It starts numbering at line 10 and continues in increments of 10. AUTO p,q starts numbering at line p and continues in increments of q. Other forms: AUTO ,q   AUTO p, and AUTO.

BGET#F   get a byte from file
BGET#p gets a byte from the file with channel number p.

BPUT#F   put a byte into file
BPUT#p puts a byte into the file with channel number p.

CALL   transfer control to a machine code subroutine
CALL p calls a section of machine code at address p. Hex
numbers can be used for p if preceded by &, for example: CALL
&FE00, and CALL Display,A,X,Y.

CHAIN
CHAIN"s" causes the file "s" to be loaded and run. It clears all
variables except integer variables (%). Examples include CHAIN(A$),
CHAINA$, CHAIN"histograms".

CHR$ character string
CHR$(p) gives the single character string whose ASCII code is p.
If p is too large, the least significant byte is used. Examples
include: CHR$(A), CHR$A, CHR$32.

CLEAR
CLEAR causes certain variables - including string variables and
arrays - to be cleared. It does not clear or affect integer variables
A% to Z%.

CLOSE#
CLOSE# p informs the system that the file with channel number
p is no longer required. CLOSE# 0 closes all files.

CLG   clear the graphics screen
CLG clears the screen of all graphics.

CLS   clear the text screen
CLS clears the screen of all text.

COLOUR
COLOURp sets the foreground or background colour for future
text. It does not affect existing text. p takes a value from 0 to 1,
3 or 15, depending on the graphics mode. The relationship between
p and the corresponding colour is described in section 7.2.

COS   cosine
COS(p) or COSp gives the cosine of p where p is in radians.

COUNT
COUNT gives the number of characters printed since the last new
line.

DATA
DATA p,q,r,. . stores numerical and string values in a program.

DEF   define
DEF is part of the statement which declares a user function or
user procedure. Examples are DEF FNmean(A,B,C), DEF PROCcalc_
areas(X,Y).

DEG   degrees
DEG(p) or DEGp gives the degree equivalent of p radians.

DELETE
DELETE p,q deletes lines p to q inclusive.

DIM   dimension of an array
DIM is part of a statement which declares an array. The
dimensions of the array are given in brackets, as for example: DIM
Num(22),Names$(3,4), A%(10,2).

DIV   integer division of whole numbers
Supplied numbers are converted to integers. Then division takes
place. The result is given as an integer value, e.g. 7 DIV 2 is 3.

DRAW
DRAW x,y draws a line, starting from the point given in the
previous graphics statement, to the point with coordinates x and y.

ELSE
ELSE is part of an IF . . THEN . . ELSE statement. It can also
be used in ON . . GOTO . . ELSE and in ON . . GOSUB . . ELSE.
For example: IF A<B THEN PRINT"Too low" ELSE PRINT"OK", or
ON A + B GOTO 100,200,250 ELSE END, or ON X GOSUB 1000,
20000 ELSE PRINT"not enough".

END
END causes a program to cease execution. It may appear in more
than one place in a program. Its use is optional at the end of a
program.

ENDPROC   end procedure
ENDPROC marks the end of a procedure and resets all LOCAL
variables to their original values.

ENVELOPE
ENVELOPE defines envelopes of sound produced using the SOUND
statement.

EOF#
EOF#p has a value -1 if the end of file p has been reached;
otherwise 0.

EOR exclusive or
EOR is an 'exclusive OR' Boolean operation between two integers.

ERL   error line number
ERL gives the line number of the line where the last error
occurred.

ERR error
ERR gives the error number for the last error.

EVAL evaluate
EVAL allows a mathematical expression to be entered as a string, for example in an INPUT statement. It evaluates the expression. For example, if A\$ = "210^x + 25*COS(Y)", then Z = EVAL A\$ is equivalent to the program line Z = 210^x + 25*COS(Y). This also works for string expressions.

EXP exponent
EXP(p) gives the exponential e raised to the power p.

EXT# extent
EXT# p gives the length of the file on channel p.

FN function
FN announces user-declared functions. Such a function may be many lines long and ends with = followed by a string or numeric quantity. For example: DEF FNmean(A,B,C), DEF FNsearch(A\$,B\$).

FOR
FOR is used at the start of a FOR . . NEXT loop.

GCOL
GCOL sets the current graphics foreground or background colour and action.

GET
GET gives a numerical value from the next character available from the input stream, keyboard, cassette or RS423. It waits until it is successful. For example: Num = GET.

GET\$
GET\$ behaves like GET but returns a string value.

GOSUB go to a subroutine
GOSUB p calls a subroutine starting at line p. The subroutine finishes with RETURN which causes execution to continue at the statement following GOSUB p.

GOTO go to a line number
GOTO p causes the execution of the program to jump to line number p, which may be given as a number or a variable.

HIMEM high memory
HIMEM is a pseudo variable which sets/gives the maximum address used by BASIC. For example Num = HIMEM, HIMEM = HIMEM + 1000.

IF
IF precedes a condition in an IF . . THEN statement. For
example: IF ans$ = "YES" THEN 100   IF G=1 THEN PRINT"hello".

INKEY   input the number of the key pressed
INKEY(p) or INKEYp gives the key pressed in the following p
centiseconds. If no key is pressed within this time, it returns -1.

INKEY$ input the character pressed on the keyboard
INKEY$(p) behaves like INKEY except that it returns a string
value.

INPUT   put information into the computer
INPUT p,p$ reads in values entered from the current input
stream, keyboard or cassette. Examples include INPUT
A,B,C,"Name"N$,D,d.

INPUT#
INPUT# is similar to INPUT except it takes its value from the
current file system.

INPUT LINE
INPUT LINE p$ is similar to INPUT except that it uses a new
line for each item. Each entered line is taken exactly as it is,
spaces, punctuation marks etc.

INSTR   in string
INSTR(Long$,Short$,p) gives the position of string Short$ in the
string Long$, with the search starting at character position p in
the Long$ string. If p is omitted, the search starts at the
beginning.

INT   integer part
INT(p) gives the integer part of the number p. For example:
INT(4.95) is 4 and INT(-5.1) is -6.

LEFT$ left string
LEFT$(A$,p) gives the left-most p characters of the string A$. If
p is larger than the length of A$, the result is A$.

LEN   length
LEN(A$) gives the length of the string A$.

LET
LET is an optional part of the assignment statement, i.e. LET
X=45 is usually abbreviated to X=45.

LIST
LIST p,q causes the current program to be listed from lines p to q inclusive. If q is omitted, listing runs from p to the end of the program. If both p and q are omitted, the whole program is listed.

LN   natural logarithm
LN(p) gives the natural logarithm of p.

LOAD
LOADA$ loads a new program in place of any previous one. Examples include LOAD"Rates", LOADB$, LOAD"histogram".

LOCAL
LOCAL p,q$ declares p, q$ and any other listed variables as local to that function or procedure. The original values are restored at the end of the function or procedure.

LOG   logarithm
LOG(p) or LOGp gives the logarithm of p to the base 10.

LOMEM   low memory
LOMEM is a pseudo variable which sets/gives the position in memory where BASIC stores its variables etc.

MID$
MID$(A$,p,q) gives the q characters in the string A$, starting at character position p. If q is omitted or too large, it gives the whole string from character position p onwards.

MOD   modulus
MOD is a binary operation giving the remainder of an integer division, e.g. A MOD B.

MODE   graphics mode
MODE p sets the graphics mode to p.

MOVE
MOVE p,q causes the current graphics position to be set to x=p and y=q. It can give the starting position for a line produced by DRAW x,y.

NEW
NEW initializes BASIC for a new program to be typed in. It clears any previous program in readiness.

NEXT
NEXT is part of the FOR . . NEXT construction.

NOT
NOT is a Boolean operation between two binary numbers.

OLD
OLD recovers a program after NEW has been entered, provided no new program lines have been entered since.

ON
ON facilitates multiway switching or error trapping. Examples included: ON X GOTO 10,100,350,35, ON X GOSUB 1000,2000, ON ERROR GOTO 500.

OPENIN   open file for input from cassette or disc
OPENIN"file" gives the channel number of the file opened for reading. If the file does not exist it gives 0.

OPENOUT   open file for output to cassette or disc
OPENOUT"file" gives the file number opened for writing. If the file already exists, material is appended; otherwise a new file is created.

OR
OR is a Boolean operation between the binary version of two integer numbers. Its usage in IF . . THEN statements is similar to that in everyday English.

PAGE
PAGE is a pseudo variable which gives/sets the start in memory for the current BASIC program. It allows a number of BASIC programs to be kept in memory at the same time.

PI
PI is a constant which BASIC takes as 3.14159265.

PLOT
PLOT p,x,y writes graphics. p controls whether points or lines or triangular areas are to be drawn and whether the coordinates x,y are absolute from the graph origin or relative to the previous x,y. Its value may be calculated from Table 7.2 in the main text.

POINT
POINT(x,y) gives the colour number of the point x,y. If it is not on the screen, it returns -1.

POS   position
POS gives the horizontal character position of the cursor on the screen. The first column is zero.

PRINT
PRINT p and PRINTq$ prints p and q$ repectively to the screen. PRINT# p causes all items in the following list to be written to the file p. Writing is continued onto the end of the present file p. All numeric values are written as five bytes of binary real data

and all strings are written as the bytes of the string followed by a return, e.g. PRINT#F,a,Name$,Num.

PROC   procedure
PROC must be used as the first four letters of the name of a user-defined procedure, such as DEF PROCcrosses(N).

PTR#   pointer (for disc systems only)
PTR# p is a pseudo variable which gives/sets the next byte to be transferred to or from file p. For example: PTR#F = PTR#F + 10.

RAD   radian
RAD(p) or RADp gives the radian equivalent of p degrees.

READ
READ instructs the computer to read in one or more variable values. Values are assigned to the variables by reading from DATA statements. If a string is encountered where a numerical value is expected then VAL("string") is assigned.

REM   remark
REM causes the rest of the program line to be ignored. It is useful for writing comments into a program to explain its operation and to divide the program up visually into parts.

RENUMBER
RENUMBER p,q causes the lines of a program to be renumbered starting at line number p with increments of q. If p or q or both are omitted, they are assumed to be 10.

REPEAT
REPEAT is the first word of the REPEAT . . UNTIL loop. These loops may be nested to a depth of 15.

RESTORE
RESTORE p sets the line number p of the DATA statement from which values will be taken using the next READ statement. p may be a number or a variable.

RETURN
RETURN ends a subroutine. It causes execution of the program to return to the statement following the most recent GOSUB.

RIGHT$ right string
RIGHT$(A$,p) gives the right-most p characters of the string A$.

RND
RND(p) gives a value which depends on the value of p. For p=1 it gives a random number between 0 and 1. For p>1 it gives a random number between 1 and p.

RUN
RUN causes a program to start executing from the beginning, all
the variables except integers being set to zero. It also causes a
program to be reexecuted.

SAVE
SAVE"s" causes the current program to be saved - on cassette or
disc - under the name "s". For example: SAVE"Word_pro",
SAVE"Star_treck".

SGN sign
SGN(p) gives -1 if p is negative, 0 if it is zero and +1 if it is
positive.

SIN sine
SIN(p) or SINp gives the sine of p where p is in radians.

SOUND
SOUND causes the computer to emit sounds, e.g. SOUND
&HSFC,amplitude/envelope,pitch,duration.

SPC space
SPC(p) can be used in a PRINT or INPUT statement where it
causes p spaces to be printed.

SQR square root
SQR(p) gives the square root of p.

STEP
STEP is the part of the FOR . . NEXT loop which specifies the
size of the step to be added to the loop variable each time the
loop is completed. If it is omitted, a step of 1 is assumed. For
example: FOR J=1 TO 7 STEP 0.2.

STOP
STOP causes the execution of the program to stop. It has the
same effect as END except that it causes a message indicating the
line number at which the program stopped running.

STR# string
STR# converts a number to the equivalent string representation,
e.g. STR$(132.5) has the value "132.5".

STRING
STRING$(p,q$) gives p lots of string q$ joined with no intervening
spaces.

TAB
TAB(p), used in a PRINT statement, causes any further printing to
begin at column p, moving onto the next line if necessary. TAB(p,q)

causes the cursor to move to character position p in line q.

TAN   tangent
TAN(p) or TANp gives the tangent of p where p is in radians.

THEN
THEN is part of the IF . . THEN structure.

TIME
TIME is a pseudo variable which gives/sets the time measured by the real-time clock in centiseconds.

TO
TO is part of the FOR . . NEXT loop structure.

TRACE
TRACE ON turns on the program-execution trace facilities.
TRACE OFF turn off the program-execution trace facilities.
TRACE p turns on the program-execution trace facilities from line p onwards.

UNTIL
UNTIL is part of the REPEAT . . UNTIL structure.

USR   user
USR has a value given by a user-written machine code routine.

VAL   value
VAL gives the numerical value for a string consisting of numbers. For example: X=VAL(A$)   Y=VAL("22").

VDU
VDU allows a following list of values to be sent to the operating system.

VPOS   vertical position of the cursor
VPOS gives the line in which the cursor is located, counting from line 0 at the top of the screen.

WIDTH
WIDTH p sets the character count before a new line is started.

Index

ABS 119
absolute value 119
ACS 118
addition 27
addressable points 79,80
addressing pixels 79,80
amplitude 167,168,174
AND 42,82,119
angular functions 117,118
animation 93,99-109,164-166
apostrophe 17
array 111,112
    one-dimensional 111,112,115
    two-dimensional 115
ASCII-codes 133-135,162
ASN 118
AR 172,173
attack rate 172,173
ATN 118
AUTO 9

binary arithmetic 81-83
binary numbers 161,162,165
BPUT 155
brackets 27
branching 37-49,53
    conditional 39
    unconditional 39
break key 3,5
byte 152,155-157

caps lock 3,5
caps lock key 4,
caps lock light 3
cassette tape 66,151
*CAT 66
channel 168,170
character
    backspace 163
    composite 162-163
    programmable 161
    line-feed 163
    matrix 161
    underline 20
    user-defined 160-162

The Authors

Neil Cryer obtained his PhD in physics at the University of Exeter in 1961, and is now a lecturer at Chelsea College, University of London where he teaches physics and microprocessor applications. He is a joint founder of the West London Personal Computer Club and a committee member of the Association of London Computer Clubs. He is a regular contributor of articles and reviews to the magazine **Personal Computer World.**

 Pat Cryer graduated in physics and mathematics at the University of Exeter in 1960, and is a qualified teacher and industrial training officer. She was a field-researcher for a major international computer company, evaluating the effectiveness of training materials with customers, and has acted as a consultant on the production of training materials. She is the co-ordinator and editor for the Society for Research into Higher Education working group to produce materials to support the training and development of university teachers. She is engaged on research for a PhD at the Institute for Educational Technology, University of Surrey.